A SERIES FOR THE WORLD

1992

World Series

WOODFORD PRESS, *San Francisco*

Produced in collaboration with
MAJOR LEAGUE BASEBALL PROPERTIES INC.

AN OFFICIAL PUBLICATION OF MAJOR LEAGUE BASEBALL

CONTENTS

1992 World Series

A SERIES

FOR THE

WORLD

Baseball's First
International
Fall Classic

A SERIES FOR THE WORLD
Baseball's First International Fall Classic

Art Direction and Design
Laurence J. Hyman

Editor
Jon Rochmis

Photography Editor
Dennis Desprois

Associate Art Director
Jim Santore

Marketing Director
David Lilienstein

Associate Designer
Todd Everett

Editorial Assistants
Leah Katz
Neil Rabin
Katy Wilcoxen

Writers	Photographers
W.P. Kinsella	Stephen Green (crew chief)
Furman Bisher	Jon Blacker
Dave Perkins	Barry Colla
	Beth Hansen
	David Lilienstein
	V.J. Lovero
	Ron Modra
	Mickey Palmer
	Manny Rubio
	Chuck Solomon
	Jerry Wachter
	Michael Zagaris

Produced in collaboration with and licensed by
MAJOR LEAGUE BASEBALL PROPERTIES, INC.

Manager, Publishing
Michael Bernstein

Supervisor, Publishing
Cynthia McManus

ISBN: 0-942627-05-9
Library of Congress Catalog Card Number: 92-62942

First Printing: December 1992
Printed and bound in the United States of America

This book was made possible with the generous assistance of Nutmeg Mills.

All photographs appearing in *A SERIES FOR THE WORLD* were shot exclusively on Film.

Film processing was kindly provided for this project by New Lab, San Francisco.

Special thanks to: Phoenix Communications, *San Francisco Examiner, San Francisco Chronicle*

PRE-GAME

And then there were two. Two countries, two cities, two teams: the finalists from the long season competing for one World Championship. The Atlanta Braves and Toronto Blue Jays had different styles and different philosophies, but there were several similarities too. One of the major ones was that they both required minor miracles in the playoffs to advance to the World Series. But then, miracles usually play a role in championship seasons.

Scenes from the Deep South span several generations but the same provincial message. Left, two fans wait in front of a striking statue of the great Georgia Peach, Ty Cobb.

The Native American motif gets worked over from practically every angle as the World Series is about to begin, from fans wearing makeshift headdresses, hardcore supporters building teepees, and a few getting their arms warmed up by doing the Chop. But there's no escaping modern technology in 1992.

The distinctive Blue Jays logo can be seen everywhere in Toronto as fans clearly display their preference. That their team defeated a long-standing nemesis, the Oakland Athletics, to qualify for the World Series makes it that much sweeter. Opposite, sold-out Atlanta-Fulton County Stadium, site of the first two games.

Signs of the season: It's a Classic,
and it happens every Fall.

Deep inside the stadiums, shielded from the fans' view, are the teams' clubhouses where players prepare for games in a variety of ways. Players get to the ballpark several hours before the gates open, and the clubhouse becomes their private domain, social area and business office, all in one.

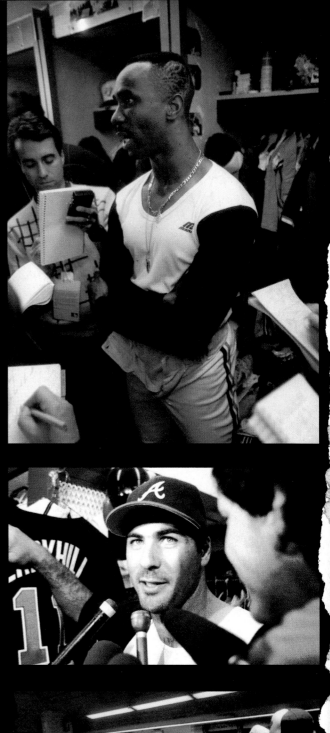

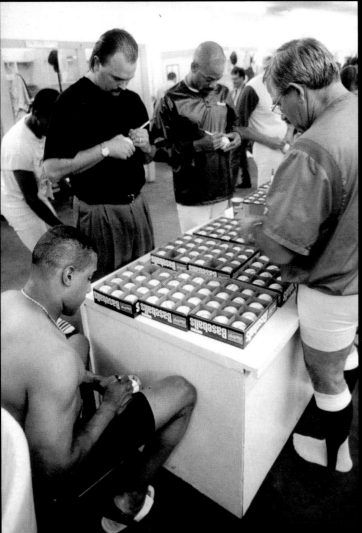

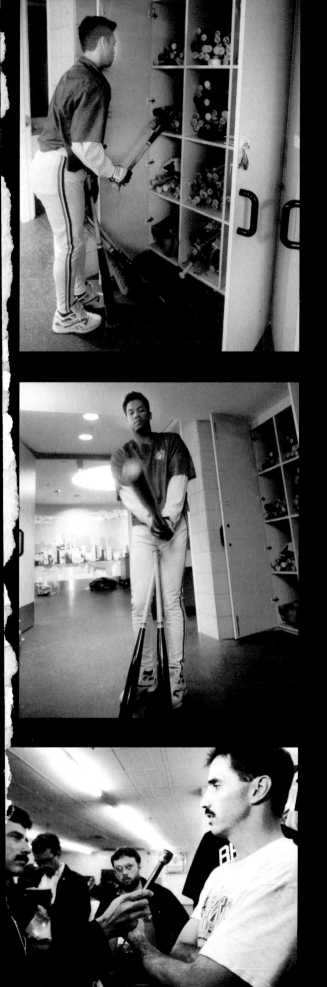

Crossing The Border

by W. P. Kinsella

The Toronto Blue Jays have just won the 1992 World Series championship. The celebrating ballplayers form a jubilant heap, wriggling like human squid in front of the pitcher's mound. As I watch the festivities from the stands it strikes me that I am viewing the most millionaires in one pile since the S&L owners went on trial.

"Does that sort of thing bother you?" I'm often asked. The astronomical salaries, players fluttering from one franchise to another, lured by larger and larger piles of cash, the ever-increasing ticket prices, or the fact that one of baseball's national treasures, George Brett, he of 3,000 hits, has signed to promote an Elvis Presley trading card.

My answer is always, "No."

If baseball is religion, which it may well be, I would be Reform rather than Orthodox. I favor the Designated Hitter Rule. I'm agreeable to domed stadiums in areas where the climate is intemperate. And while I consider myself somewhat pure of heart where traditional baseball is involved, for the good of all concerned, I'm not above unlatching the chastity belt while the Lord of the Manor is absent.

*　　　*　　　*

Toronto the Good. Atlanta the Beautiful. The two teams who most deserve to be in the Fall Classic. The two teams with the best farm systems in baseball.

Toronto, a baseball hotbed, drew more than four million fans in 1991 and 1992, while Atlanta, which two years ago couldn't outdraw a senior citizen soccer game, attracted in excess of three million fans.

The first World Series to cross a geopolitical border. The first World Series championship to leave the United States. The Jays are the first expansion team to win a World Series since Kansas City in 1985. But Toronto is no baseball upstart. The city has a colorful baseball history. In 1914, 19-year-old Babe Ruth hit his first professional home run in Toronto, wearing the uniform of the Providence Grays, in a game against the Toronto Maple Leafs of the International League.

Unlike many major cities, Toronto is clean, stable, non-violent, with a vibrant and bustling downtown. Show-business personality Peter Ustinov described Toronto as "New York City run by the Swiss."

Toronto's SkyDome is a wonder of the modern world. The retractable roof covers eight acres and weighs an unbelievable 19 million pounds, and at its apex stands 31 stories above the playing field. The longest home run hit in SkyDome, if popped straight up, would not hit the roof.

Atlanta, home of Coca-Cola, the 1996 Summer Olympics and Margaret Mitchell, creator of *Gone With the Wind,* is a city still pursuing its first major championship in any sport. Atlanta's air is soft as a baby's cheek, scented by peach blossoms in spring and an abundance of semi-tropical blooms year round. A statue of all-time home run leader Hank Aaron stands on guard outside Fulton County Stadium with its deep, grassy playing field. Baseball as she is meant to be played. The thrill of the grass.

19

Atlanta has a secret past; it was originally named Terminus, because that was where the railroad ended, and later Marthasville, after the daughter of a self-important politician. Atlanta is the feminine of Atlantic. Macy's Department Store installed the first escalator in the South, one largely ignored by Atlantans unused to such newfangled gadgetry. The escalator was eventually dismantled and moved to a more appreciative city.

*　　　*　　　*

GAME ONE: A lesson in the long ball. Joe Carter's home run accounts for Toronto's solitary score, while one reckless pitch from Jack Morris permits light-hitting catcher Damon Berryhill to create all three of Atlanta's runs with one swing of the stick.

*　　　*　　　*

Some journalists want to see this first international series as a clash of ideologies. Many, particularly in Canada, want to compare this series with the historic Canada-Russia hockey showdown of 1972. But there is essentially no clash of ideologies between Canada and the United States, no rivalry except the friendly one of two great baseball teams from two great nations, challenging one another.

During the series, I was taken to task on a Canadian radio talk show for stating my belief that Canadians and Americans are essentially interchangeable. My conviction is based on 20 years of extended travel in both countries. As it says on the Peace Arch at the Blaine, Washington/White Rock, British Columbia border crossing, near my home, *We Are Children of a Common Mother.*

In spite of some members of the press trying to create unwarranted controversy, there was never real animosity between fans on either side, and after the Blue Jays won Game Six in Atlanta, the Braves fans, after the initial stunned silence, applauded in appreciation as the Blue Jays celebrated on the field.

The better team won.

Atlanta fans acknowledged the victory, and I'm sure Toronto fans would have done the same had the situation been reversed.

*　　　*　　　*

If this is the first international competition, why have we been calling it the World Series for 89 years? I always assumed that the World Series had global connotations, and was surprised to learn the name derives from a long-defunct newspaper, the *New York World*, which sponsored the first meeting between National and American League champions in 1903. What if it had been the *New York Times*? Would it be known as the Times Series today?

*　　　*　　　*

GAME TWO: The flag incident. The Canadian flag is carried upside down during pre-game ceremonies. Certainly no malice aforethought was involved. An easy enough mistake by someone unfamiliar with the Canadian flag, for in the natural world leaves do hang *down* from tree branches. Also, keep in mind the Deep South is still an insular society where local history is proudly taught, while the outside world often receives scant attention. Many Georgians have never seen the Canadian flag before, a goodly number have only a vague idea of Canada's precise geographic location. A cashier, taking my credit card, asked, "British Columbia? Is that in South America?"

In Toronto, prior to Game Three, the flag incident is handled with incredible skill and diplomacy. In an emotional pre-game ceremony a United States color guard carries the Canadian flag, while Royal Canadian Mounted Police display the Stars and Stripes, defusing once and for all what could have been an ongoing and ugly episode.

Later in Game Two, Kelly Gruber earns the wrath of Atlanta fans with his "Chop You" gesture as he rounds the bases. Ed Sprague's come-from-behind home run is a decisive point in the series, for it turns the tide away from Atlanta (without it Atlanta would have gone into Toronto with a two-game lead) to give Toronto an advantage they never relinquish.

More importantly, Game Two is where Toronto shows its maturity as a ballclub. In the 1985 League Championship Series in Kansas City, an incredibly bad call by first base Umpire Don Denkinger broke

20

Toronto's spirit. The Blue Jays folded up and blew a 3-1 lead in games. The same could easily have happened in Game Two when Roberto Alomar, clearly safe at home plate, is called out, costing the Jays a run.

In 1992, instead of collapsing, the Blue Jays show great fortitude by putting the bad call behind them and coming back to eventually win the game.

*   *   *

As a baseball fan, my loyalties are divided. An uncomfortable situation. I am happier when I have one team to love and one team to pull against. If only the Jays were playing the Mets, or Atlanta facing the Yankees. I want both teams to win. I'm a Canadian, a fan of the Jays in the American League East, but my wife Ann Knight and I are also unpaid Associate Scouts for the Atlanta Braves. We have many friends in the Braves organization. We've watched Steve Avery since he was a star high school pitcher. Yes, we want the impossible. We want both teams to win. No matter how magical the series, that is not going to happen.

*   *   *

GAME THREE: Crossing the border. History is made. Never before has a World Series game been played outside the United States. A proud and memorable moment for Canada. With the first pitch of Game Three baseball memory is forever altered.

Already 1992 seems to be a catchers' series. The men behind the tools of ignorance—Borders, Sprague and Berryhill—have so far had major impact, while Atlanta's Francisco Cabrera, the hero of the League Championship Series, is the anticipatory joy of Atlanta fans, who hope that at the appropriate moment he will be able to duplicate his LCS heroics.

The 1992 Series is Canada's in every way. Canadian astronaut Steven MacLean carries a Blue Jays cap into space, and accepts good-natured wagers from his American counterparts.

Canada's sweetheart, Anne Murray, sings the national anthem.

The defensive play of the series takes place when Toronto center fielder Devon White, flying like an angel, snatches a Dave Justice fly ball and crashes into the fence, saving a three-run home run, leaving the imprint of his body in the padded blue wall. To the imaginative fan—the true believer in the wedding of baseball and magic—the image is still visible innings later, faint as a veronica.

On the same play Toronto is denied what would have been the second triple play in World Series history, when Umpire Bob Davidson misses a call at second base. Toronto is so thrilled with Devon White's miracle catch, one that ranks right up there with Willie Mays and Al Gionfriddo, that it is not as outraged about being denied the triple play as it would have been in other circumstances. What counts is the Jays got out of the inning without giving up a run.

The strategy that decides the series is Toronto Manager Cito Gaston's decision to use a fourth starter, left-hander Jimmy Key. This allows a long-rested Key to pitch Game Four, leaving Game Five and Six starters Morris and David Cone to pitch on four days' rest. Atlanta, on the other hand, decides to go with its young starting pitchers on three days' rest. While Smoltz and Glavine acquitted themselves adequately, Avery needs four days between starts, and is a much better pitcher on five days' rest. It might have been an entirely different series had Atlanta Manager Bobby Cox made Gaston's choice. What if Pete Smith started Game Four? Win or lose, a rested Smoltz, Avery and Glavine would have been available for Games Five, Six and Seven.

Now that he has won the World Championship, Cito Gaston may finally get his due as a great manager. The Toronto press has been incredibly unkind to Gaston, often acting like a pack of curs snapping at a burglar's ankles. Gaston is a very talented manager and one of the finest gentlemen in the game. He deserves better.

*   *   *

Is there always going to be a World Series? Does baseball have insurmountable problems? Is the game any less exciting because of astronomical player salaries and slow games? Does it take away from the enchantment of the game that players are now businessmen, instead of men playing a boy's game for fun rather than profit? Once again, I don't think so. Many players are overpaid, but they are also speedier and better conditioned than ever before. In baseball as in real life, what goes around comes around. The owners exploited the players for donkey's years. Now, the tables are turned. I feel it will all work out. Perhaps a salary cap will have to be instituted in order for smaller markets to survive and compete.

Television has much to do with the slowness of the games. However, I think a rule forbidding the batter to step out between pitches would be beneficial, as well as strictly enforcing the 20-second time limit between pitches.

*   *   *

GAME FOUR: Toronto goes up 3-1 in games. The high points of the contest are two images of Toronto third baseman Kelly Gruber. (Is there any major-league ballplayer who shows more hustle?) The first is of him sliding chin-first across home plate, his face full of surprise and pain, and later we see him in full flight, making a bare-handed play on a ground ball, throwing to first base for a game-saving put-out.

Second-guessers will wonder for a long time why Bobby Cox didn't pinch hit for Jeff Blauser, who made the final out with the tying run in scoring position.

*   *   *

The chicken or the egg syndrome: The lighter side of the series was accentuated by a columnist speculating on whether baseball players develop broad backsides because of playing baseball, or do they become baseball players because they have broad backsides?

*   *   *

In Canada, where a bitter political debate raged over constitutional change, the Prime Minister, Brian Mulroney, tried to use the World Series to political advantage by suggesting that a Blue Jays victory could lead to warm and fuzzy feelings of patriotism and national unity, thus assuring a win for the YES side of the referendum, the Prime Minister's side. His ploy failed. The NO side won a resounding victory two days later, in spite of the Blue Jays' triumph.

*   *   *

Atlanta's sometimes controversial Tomahawk Chop is a phenomenon that has to be experienced. The Chop has little to do with baseball, nothing to do with Native Americans, and everything to do with the religiosity of the Deep South that permeates the air like the scent of magnolia in the ever-present humidity.

Experiencing the mesmerizing chant that accompanies the Chop, the swaying bodies, the rhythm of the rising and falling arms, conjuring up not baseball images, or sports images at all, but the wild-eyed enthusiasm of a no-holds-barred, fire-and-brimstone, roll-in-the-aisles-for-Jesus, double-helpin'-of-the-Lord, speaking-in-tongues, tent-meeting revival. One might substitute for the hands and arms engaged in the Chop, the arms raised in ecstatic praise; for the babbling chant accompanying the Chop, zealous riverside glossolalia.

I, who pride myself on staying aloof in such situations, of always remaining the analyst, became totally caught up in the fervor of Game Six, wishing, if not praying, for a seventh game. The adrenaline flowed like whisky through my veins. I ended up chopping with the best of them, and as the intensity of the game increased, keeping my eyes attached to the Atlanta batters in the bottom of the 11th—Blauser, Berryhill, Belliard, Hunter and Nixon—repeating, "You can see the ball clearly. You can see the ball clearly."

*   *   *

Although I've seen hundreds of major league baseball games, and a few League Championship encounters, Game Five in Toronto and Game Six in Atlanta are my first live World Series games.

Is the atmosphere different? You bet it is. Prior the games, each stadium is like a classroom just before a crucial examination, everyone giddy with anticipation. Minor events which are usually avoided or ignored, like player introductions and national anthems, take on new importance. The excitement and enthusiasm are catching as pink eye.

I usually bring a book with me which I read between innings and during pitching changes. No time for that at the World Series. Every fan hangs on every pitch. This late in such a short series, one team always has its back to the wall, and that tension hangs in the air, giving every action, no matter how mundane, a new significance.

*   *   *

GAME FIVE: The Braves close the gap in the only game that was not a heart-stopper. Veteran Lonnie Smith whacks a grand slam to break the game open for the Braves.

The best line from a player this series came from Jack Morris after his second loss. He allowed as how, "Atlanta is in deep trouble. I'm not gonna pitch again."

On this night, baseball suffers a major loss with the passing of Red Barber, the consummate radio broadcaster, whose silky voice introduced millions of Americans to baseball and to such immortal phrases as "tearing up the peapatch."

The defensive play of the game was Devon White's gunning down Mark Lemke at the plate.

The kiss of death award: Before Game Five, an overzealous bureaucrat at Toronto City Hall released details of the next day's victory parade, if Toronto won. Baseball players—being only slightly less superstitious than those who divine the future from gopher entrails, and see Elvis Presley's silhouette on the doors of abandoned refrigerators—immediately panicked. For Toronto, defeat became a self-fulfilling prophecy.

*   *   *

Why do I write about baseball? I am often asked. A great deal of quality fiction has been written about baseball, several excellent baseball movies have been produced, yet virtually no lasting fiction or movies of quality have been forthcoming for all other sports combined.

My answer is that baseball is particularly conducive to fiction writing because of the open-endedness of the game. The other sports are twice enclosed, first by rigid playing boundaries, second by time limits. As we all know there is no time limit on a baseball game, while on the true baseball field the foul lines diverge forever, eventually taking in a good part of the universe, which makes for myth and larger-than-life characters. That's what fiction writers spend all their lives searching for. In baseball there is theoretically no distance a great hitter couldn't strike the ball, or a great outfielder could run to retrieve it. It doesn't matter what spectacular feats athletes like Michael Jordan or Wayne Gretzky perform, they are still trapped on tightly enclosed playing surfaces, and it is almost impossible to create mythology from such a small base.

*   *   *

GAME SIX: Four hours plus of changing fortunes, suspense, religious fervor, heartbreak, elation and magnificent baseball. The game was delayed some 15 minutes when Presidential candidate Ross Perot purchased network time to air his views. How could this happen? Was Perot paying more for his time than the sponsors of the World Series?

When Mike Timlin scooped up Otis Nixon's bunt and tossed to first to end the game, and the series, in the bottom of the 11th inning, even Blue Jays fans were almost drained of adrenaline.

The several turning points in the final game: When Terry Pendleton struck out in the bottom of the fifth with men on second and third. When Gant flied out in the ninth with the winning run at third. When Francisco Cabrera lined out to Candy Maldonado, a couple of feet higher or to one side or the other and there would have been a Game Seven. And, of course, Nixon not taking at least one pitch from Timlin, who had not worked in ages, and is not known as a really effective pitcher, and who, entering the game in such a critical situation, must have had butterflies the size of King Kong dancing about in his chest.

Best Signs: A Toronto fan with a card reading CHOP PHOOEY! Sign in SkyDome—WINFIELD OF DREAMS. Appropriate that Dave Winfield, the oldest player in the series, should send a screamer over third base in the 11th inning to score the winning runs, silencing the 50,000-plus Atlanta fans. Winfield, all season long, was an inspiration to both his team and the Toronto fans. It is only appropriate that at the

23

victory celebration in SkyDome, Winfield was asked to give the signal unveiling the pennant reading 1992 WORLD SERIES CHAMPS.

Around 50,000 Toronto fans, as if following an invisible pied piper, perhaps the Ghost of Baseball Past juggling and cartwheeling down Yonge Street, filled SkyDome to view Game Six on the giant screen.

After the Blue Jays triumph, 400,000 fans swarmed the streets of downtown Toronto. In keeping with Canadian tradition, the celebration was raucous, but not riotous. The best line of the series came from a West Coast writer who speculated that celebrating Toronto fans rushed into the streets to pick up litter and hug policemen.

Dave Winfield summed up the first international World Series when he said, "America's game is now going to Canada for a while."

GAME ONE

The events of Game One promised a great World Series. This was a tight, clean, errorless ballgame highlighted by the crisp starting pitching of Atlanta's Tom Glavine and Toronto's Jack Morris. Joe Carter gave the Blue Jays a 1-0 lead in the fourth inning with a home run to left field, and the Braves scored all of their runs in the sixth on catcher Damon Berryhill's three-run homer to right-center.

BRAVES 3, BLUE JAYS 1

Lovingly cleaned and manicured, Atlanta Stadium is ready for the drama ahead. Pre-game, the mood and atmosphere is loose and light-hearted. Above, Roberto Alomar has just taken his practice cuts. Former President Jimmy Carter and First Lady Rosalynn Carter visit with Jane Fonda. Opposite, managers Cito Gaston and Bobby Cox renew an old friendship. Gaston acknowledges a fan.

The battle begins. Clockwise from top left, Atlanta pitcher Tom Glavine successfully gets out of the first inning. Terry Pendleton and Candy Maldonado take their turns at bat. Jack Morris follows through. Sid Bream drives a single up the middle in the sixth inning.

Opposite, Joe Carter watches his leadoff home run in the fourth inning sail over the left-field wall, then calmly makes the final turn home for the Blue Jays' only run. Above, Jeff Blauser follows a pitch all the way into the catcher's mitt. After getting Pat Borders for the first out of the eighth inning, Rafael Belliard tries to complete the double play.

With the weight of the World Series hanging over their heads, Joe Carter and Candy Maldonado go about their business. Jack Morris throws out Otis Nixon to end the third. Kelly Gruber follows through at the plate.

34

Atlanta sparkles from Damon Berryhill's big blow
in Game One, a three-run homer in the sixth inning.

After a productive night at the office, Tom Glavine gets a hero's welcome from teammates and Manager Bobby Cox.

Gone With Two Wins

by Furman Bisher
Atlanta Journal-Constitution

Somehow a sense of predestination overtook Atlanta and its tomahawk-chopping, chanting constituency after the dramatically shocking fashion in which the National League playoffs had ended. One solid blow to left field by a rarely used backup catcher, slow-footed Sid Bream chugging all the way home from second, sliding under the tag of Mike Lavalliere—the oddly conformed Pittsburgh catcher—with the third run of the ninth inning, and just that suddenly, two men out, two strikes on Francisco Cabrera—Señor Last Resort from Santo Domingo—the Braves had become champions of the National League again in the seventh game of a rigorous playoff.

While Pirates sat or stood around the field of screams—Andy Van Slyke plumped down in center field—Braves and fans exploded into the outer space of ecstasy. Realizing that their American League opponents in the World Series would be the Toronto Blue Jays, untried and untested under such a crucible, it was precluded that this would be the Year of the Braves. Besides, there was the course of the Series before to call upon, when Minnesota won all four home games under its roof and Atlanta won its three home games. This time the Braves would have that home-game edge, four games on grass under nature's roof, three games in Toronto's palatial parlor. It seemed a given. Trouble was, they never got to the fourth home game, but we're getting ahead of our story.

The Braves' victory over Jack Morris in the opening game in Atlanta gave underpinning to the theory that they were predestined to become champions of the first international World Series. Hadn't Morris been their tormentor as a Twin? Hadn't he shut them out for 10 innings in 1991's seventh game and left them with a long, dismal winter? Wasn't this a good omen, proving that Jack Morris was vincible?

It was a continuation of the glorification of the most unlikely star of all, the backup catcher. The catcher is the one rolling in the dirt, his head under a plastic skull cap that makes him look as if he's headed for an execution, uniform soiled, working on his knees, usually in the bullpen warming up the next pitcher. This was Cabrera in the seventh playoff game, made eligible only on the deadline date of August 31, and who had come from Toronto three years earlier as a "player-to-be-named-later." Now it was Damon Berryhill, catching only because Greg Olson was wearing a cast from a home-plate collision.

(Two of baseball's most unusual backup catchers never played in a World Series. Moe Berg, a scholarly Princeton graduate, spoke seven languages and carried on a second career of espionage as an agent for the United States, but 15 years as a major-league reserve never included a World Series game. Arndt Jorgens, born in Norway, played on five New York Yankees teams that made the World Series during the 1930s, but never got into a game. He saw his World Series from the bullpen.)

Toronto led 1-0 on Joe Carter's home run in the fourth inning. The Blue Jays never made another dent in Tom Glavine, who matched Morris' four-hitter with one of his own. But the Braves would have to wait until the sixth inning, David Justice and Ron Gant on base, and at the plate Berryhill, the switch-hitting catcher batting on the left side. He caught an inside pitch and dispatched it over the right field fence and three runs scored. That was the end of Morris and all Glavine needed. From the fifth inning on he faced the minimum number of Blue Jays. One reached base, but Pat Borders was wiped out on a double play after a single.

"Not This Time, Jack!" *The Atlanta Journal* headlined it the next day. This was further assurance that Atlanta's sense of predestination was correct. Pay no attention to all that puffery produced by Major League Baseball's energetic staff. Such as, the city with the tallest building wins the World Series six out of 10 times, and the CN Tower in Toronto is 758 feet taller than the C&S Plaza, Atlanta's tallest.

Thus it was unnerving that Sunday night was the night of another backup catcher, but this time it was Toronto's turn. Ed Sprague is an erudite graduate of Stanford University laboring in the "tools of ignorance" as a Blue Jays rookie. Half the season he had spent on the farm in Syracuse and had been to bat just 47 times with the Blue Jays. There was only one home run on his card.

The Braves had been moving along well—firmly supporting the predestination theorists—and led at one time, 4-2, before John Smoltz surrendered a run when Roberto Alomar doubled and Dave Winfield drove him home with a single in the eighth inning. Still ahead 4-3, Manager Bobby Cox had called on Jeff Reardon, the bearded right-hander highly regarded as a "closer." John Schuerholz, the crafty general manager, had traded minor-league talent to the Boston Red Sox for Reardon August 30.

Reardon struck out Kelly Gruber to end the troublesome eighth inning, but walked pinch-hitter Derek Bell in the ninth, and that brought up Sprague to hit for the pitcher, Duane Ward, who had been incubated in the Braves' farm system. Reardon's first pitch, the first pitch Sprague has ever seen in a World Series, is one the backup catcher likes and he returns it into the left field seats. Suddenly, a 4-3 lead has become a 5-4 deficit and that's the way it ends.

"What was the scouting report on Sprague?" Cox was asked in the interview room.

"Low fastball hitter," the manager said, "and that's exactly what he hit."

Most damaging to the predestination theorists was that the Braves had lost one of their given games at home, on grass, under a natural sky. This was not augured to happen, and so their team set out to become the visitors in a World Series experience never known since the baseball grew stitches. First World Series to go through customs, first World Series to exchange currency, first World Series on foreign soil—albeit just across Lake Ontario from Buffalo. First World Series with two national anthems, each taking its turn being butchered by some improvising group or pelvic-weaving soloist at one time or another, serving to double the appreciation for Anne Murray's warm rendition of "O Canada," once we were in SkyDome, the best of the major leagues' covered halls—if indeed baseball must be played under cover.

Throughout the National League playoffs and into the World Series, a constant center of controversy had been Deion Sanders, the Braves' outfielder and also an Atlanta Falcons defensive back and kick returner. Sanders had incited Schuerholz's rancor when he tried to squeeze in a day with the Falcons in the middle of the playoffs.

"I had an agreement with him and his agent that he would give the Braves his undivided attention during the post-season," Schuerholz said.

In apparent violation, Sanders boarded a chartered jet after the Saturday night game in Pittsburgh, flew to Miami and joined the Falcons for a game against the Dolphins. Afterward, he had been so dehydrated he had to be treated with two bags of intravenous fluid, then flew back to Allegheny County Airport, where the plane landed at 8:28 p.m. The Braves and Pirates played at 8:30. Schuerholz was furious. There was some name calling, mostly through the papers, but still, more in need of a position player and a bat to come off the bench than another pitcher, Schuerholz and Cox included Sanders on the World Series roster.

Further complicating the story, after the Braves had beaten the Pirates for the pennant, Tim McCarver of CBS was on a podium in the locker room working the customary trophy awarding and ceremonial when Sanders doused him with a pail of water, not once but three times. Sanders had become offended when

McCarver, a former catcher, criticized him on-air during the playoffs for trying to fit in the Falcons gambit while the Braves were scratching and clawing for their lives. "Self-centered," McCarver called it.

Nevertheless, Sanders was among those present, and as the Series moved to SkyDome and American League rules came into effect, Sanders would move into left field against the right-handed Juan Guzman, replacing Ron Gant, who was having a dreadful Series. Sanders had started in Atlanta against David Cone, singled and scored a run. Now he turned it up a few notches, singled his first time at bat, beat out an infield hit and became the central figure in what would have been the first triple play in a World Series since Bill Wambsganss of Cleveland pulled one off by himself in 1920. But National League Umpire Bob Davidson of Altoona, Pa., made a call that he confessed the following day had been in error, and a phenomenal 400-foot triple play—from center field to first to second to third (Terry Pendleton was automatically out for passing Sanders on the basepath)—became a mere, though not necessarily routine, double play.

Pendleton had singled behind Sanders, nobody out and David Justice at bat. Justice drove Guzman's pitch to deepest center field. Devon White turned and made a leaping catch at the top of the fence, falling into the protective covering. So sure it was a hit, Pendleton took off and had already rounded second, where Sanders stood. Seeing Pendleton there, Sanders took off for third and was caught in a rundown. Gruber gave chase, and instead of flipping the ball to Alomar on the bag, lunged and caught Sanders on the heel, the part that Davidson's eyes missed. Other than depriving the world of baseball history, no real harm was done because Lonnie Smith, the designated hitter, struck out to end the inning.

Sanders wasn't through, though. He doubled in the sixth and scored the first Braves run. We were beginning to see him more as the baseball player than a curiosity, and he was only warming to the moment. So was Bobby Cox, who became so overheated at calls made on Jeff Blauser when his shortstop was at bat in the eighth that he threw a batting helmet on the field and was thrown out of the game, first such in a World Series since another Cox, Danny the pitcher of St. Louis, had been tossed during 1985's seven-game classic against Kansas City.

The Jays won 3-2 for a two-games-to-one series lead.

When Jimmy Key shut down the Braves in the fourth game, visions of the Blue Jays closing it out on their own turf began to take hold around Toronto. Manager Cito Gaston had taken a gamble with Key, the Southern-bred left-hander who had not been included in the playoff rotation, and in a nation where ice hockey is the national pastime, the baseball manager lives on tenuous terms with the natives. Once the decision worked, though, Gaston was a hero again. It was a fascinating match of managers: Cox, who had once managed the Blue Jays into the American League playoffs, and Gaston, whom Cox had given his first chance as a major-league coach. Each was careful not to reflect upon the other in their visits with the press.

Now down three games to one, the Braves had a mountain to climb, considering that only six times before had any team come back from a similar deficit to win a World Series. Not that it should seem that big of a deal. All it requires is a three-game wining streak, and championship teams do that several times during a season. Nonetheless, much is made of it in all those press communiques MLB produces.

Cox turned now to John Smoltz, his strikeout pitcher, not that he had any other choice, unless he broke his rotation and went to Pete Smith, a perfect 7-0 at the end of the season, or the veteran Charlie Leibrandt. Both had been unceremoniously dumped into the bullpen. Smoltz was not necessarily at his sharpest, but he managed to hold the Blue Jays at bay for six innings, then turned it over to Mike Stanton, the stubby left-hander who pitches from behind his right knee. By that time the Braves were in the fairly safe condition of riding on a 7-2 lead, due to a home run by Justice in the fourth inning and a long, tall, lazy arc over the wrong-field fence by Lonnie Smith that became only the third National League grand slam home run in World Series history. Once again, however, let it be pointed out here that when Sanders crossed the plate on Smith's home run, he bore the Braves' lead run. He singled again in the ninth and led all players in the series with a .500 batting average.

Toronto's hope of ending it there having failed, it was back to Atlanta, Saturday night in Atlanta Stadium for the sixth game. The game would start about 15 minutes late because of some television commitment to

Ross Perot, the Presidential candidate. It would not end until 12:50 a.m., four hours and seven minutes later, with America's parlor-watchers nodding or in the hay.

Sid Bream's oldest son is six. "He never gets a chance to see me play in the World Series," the Braves' first baseman said. "It's almost his bedtime by the time the game comes on the TV."

The climactic game began with eight innings of routine baseball, Blue Jays leading 2-1 on Candy Maldonado's home run in the fourth, Steve Avery's last inning. The young left-hander did not have his control, and Pete Smith, Mike Stanton and Mark Wohlers kept the Blue Jays in check until the Braves finally awoke from a deep sleep and tied the game in the ninth when Otis Nixon sliced a single down the left field line, scoring Jeff Blauser. Now came Charlie Leibrandt in relief, once again to suffer the humiliation of defeat when Dave Winfield, oldest man on the field, doubled home Devon White and Roberto Alomar in the 11th inning. Leibrandt had been left in to pitch to the right-handed power in the Blue Jays' order, much to the dismay of grandstand managers, who would have called in Reardon, already warmed up in the bullpen.

In the back of every mind was the pitch that Kirby Puckett hit off Leibrandt in Minneapolis in the sixth game last year. This time, it might have worked for the left-hander, a 15-game winner in season, had he not brushed White's trousers with a pitch. Alomar's single followed and Joe Carter's fly to center was the second out, but here came Winfield.

The Braves got a run back in their half of the 11th, Blauser leading again with his third hit. It ended when Nixon failed to beat out a bunt down the first-base line. A small cluster of Canadians went wild in Atlanta Stadium, where there was little left to be said or celebrated.

There were grounds for little grief. It had been a glorious season, with or without a championship flag to fly. At least the Braves could take some solace in that they joined two of baseball's distinguished dynasties, the Dodgers and the Yankees, as the only teams to lose two World Series in a row this side of the century. Destiny simply had not been with them.

1992 FALL
ATLANTA-FULTON COUNTY STAD

GAME 2

FIELD
LEVEL
$60.00
Tax Included

Braves™

VS.
ERICAN LEAGUE
CHAMPIONS

1992
World Series®

RAIN CHECK
RAIN CHECK subject to the con-
ditions set forth on back hereof.
DO NOT DETACH THIS COUPON
FRANCIS T. VINCENT, JR.
Commissioner of Baseball

FIELD
LEVEL
$60.00
Tax Included

1992   FALL   CL
ATLANTA-FULTON COUNTY

GATE   124
AISLE

GAME TWO

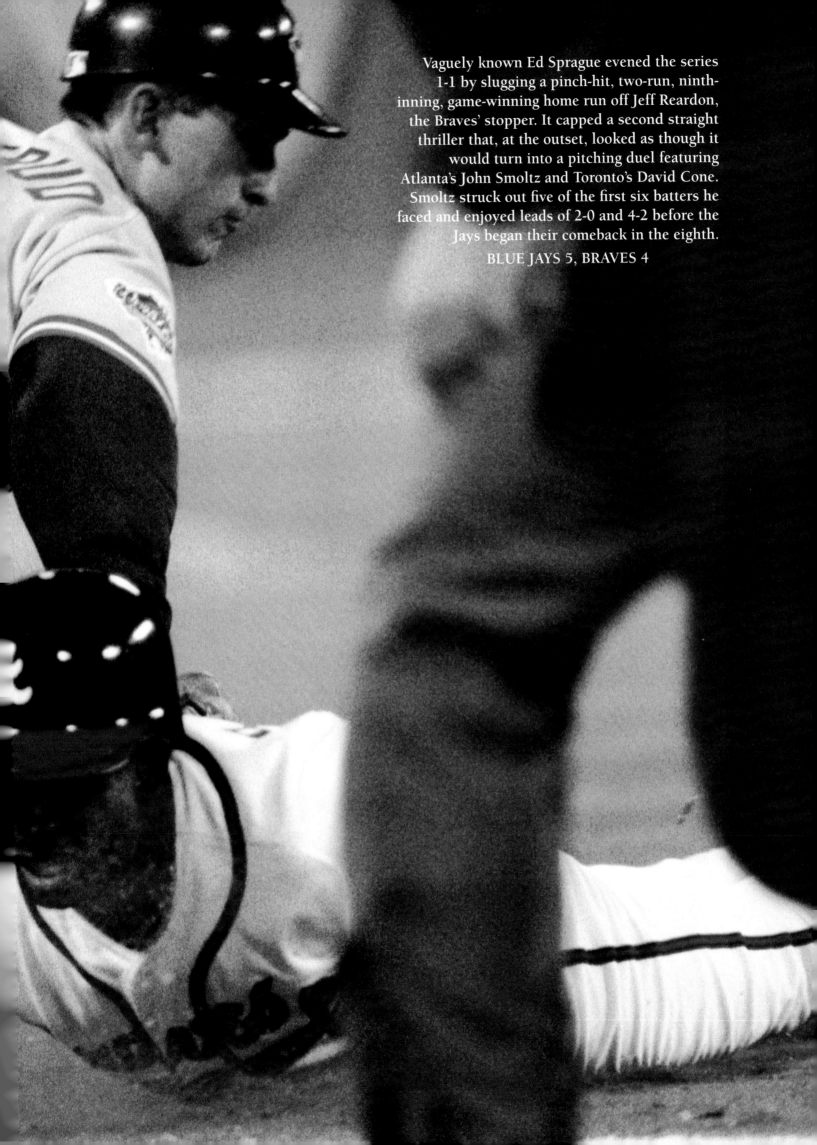

Vaguely known Ed Sprague evened the series 1-1 by slugging a pinch-hit, two-run, ninth-inning, game-winning home run off Jeff Reardon, the Braves' stopper. It capped a second straight thriller that, at the outset, looked as though it would turn into a pitching duel featuring Atlanta's John Smoltz and Toronto's David Cone. Smoltz struck out five of the first six batters he faced and enjoyed leads of 2-0 and 4-2 before the Jays began their comeback in the eighth.

BLUE JAYS 5, BRAVES 4

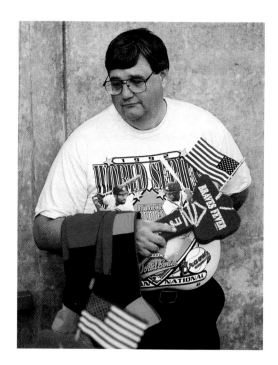

Fans come in all shapes, sizes and headdresses.

46

David Cone and the Coneheads.

As one of the Braves' chief fans surveys the scene, David Justice gets a lucky break in the second inning when Manuel Lee tries for the out at third but the throw hits Justice in the back.

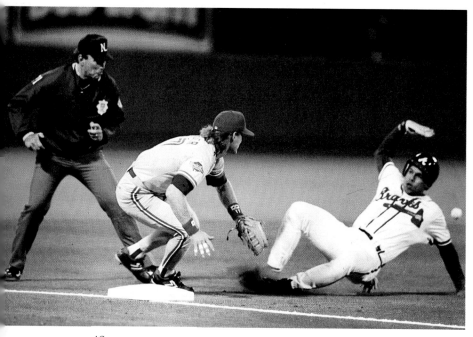

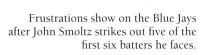

Frustrations show on the Blue Jays after John Smoltz strikes out five of the first six batters he faces.

Opposite, the first controversial call of the series. Roberto Alomar slides head-first in a bang-bang play at the plate in the fourth, but umpire Mike Reilly says John Smoltz applied the tag first. Left, Sid Bream takes a breather before scoring in the fourth. Roberto Alomar, Deion Sanders and Manuel Lee follow the unpredictable path of the play.

John Olerud sends David Justice to the track in the fifth inning. Roberto Alomar waits for his pitch. A pitching change allows time for Kelly Gruber, Manuel Lee and Alomar to discuss strategy.

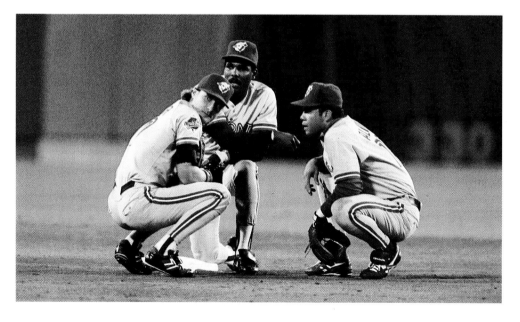

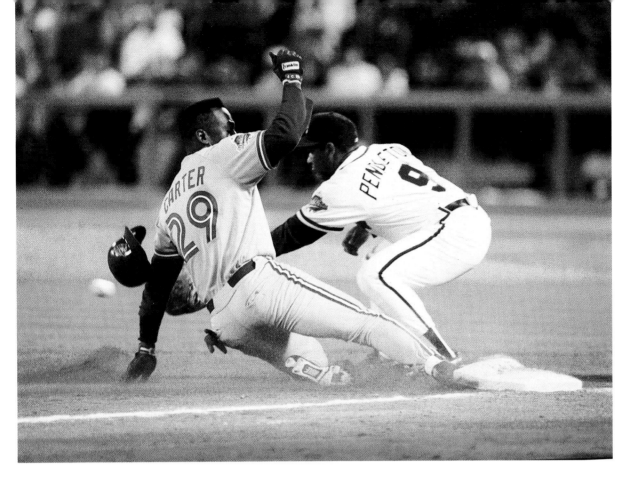

Joe Carter beats
the throw to
Terry Pendleton
at third base,
setting up Dave
Winfield's run-
scoring single
to the opposite
field.

The Shot Heard 'Round
Canada: Light-hitting Ed
Sprague's pinch-hit, two-run,
game-winning home run
against Atlanta relief ace Jeff
Reardon in the ninth inning.
Derek Bell congratulates
Sprague, Blue Jays style, with
a belly bump.

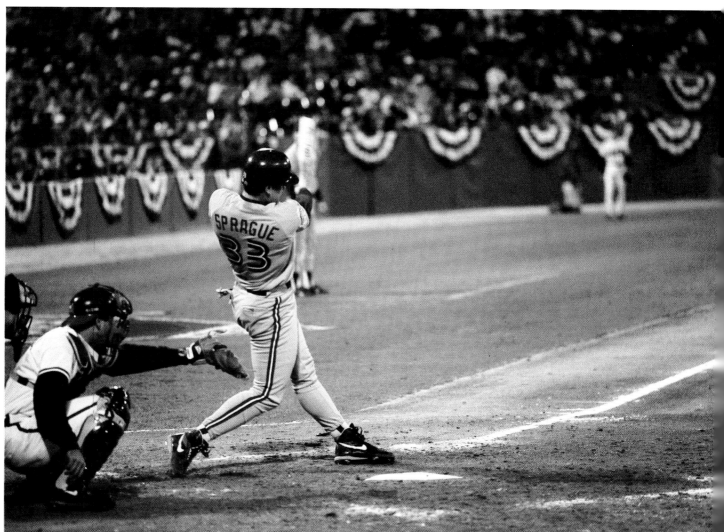

It's difficult for young fans to comprehend a Blue Jays victory in Atlanta.

GAME THREE

SKYDOME, TORONTO
October 20, 1992

*"Sometimes I just put my hands out and
hope that the ball drops in, like a magnet."*

—Devon White

The first World Series game ever played outside the United States nearly had the first World Series triple play since 1920, featuring a sensational, leaping, back-to-the-plate, against-the-wall catch by Devon White off the bat of David Justice. Toronto's Joe Carter and Kelly Gruber homered, Juan Guzman pitched masterfully, and Blue Jays fans went home happy after another ninth-inning win, this one manufactured on hits by Roberto Alomar and Candy Maldonado.

BLUE JAYS 3, BRAVES 2

The World Series gets treated to new, different looks when it crosses the border for the first time.

Canadians quickly indulge themselves in the excitement of the first international Fall Classic. But it's still the World Series, and both teams conduct themselves with quiet, respectful determination.

Preceding page, fireworks signal the start of the first World Series game ever played outside of the United States. Left, Juan Guzman's challenge: To shut down the Braves, which means containing Deion Sanders on the bases.

Pat Borders and
Kelly Gruber
would come up
with big hits, but
they also provide
tight defense for
the Jays as well
(top). Lefty Steve
Avery does what
the Braves had
hoped—silence
Toronto's bats—
but it's not enough.

The Triple Play That Wasn't: Opposite, Deion Sanders starts the fourth inning by beating out an infield single. David Justice takes a Juan Guzman pitch to the center field wall, where Devon White makes one of the great catches in World Series history. Left, Terry Pendleton passes Sanders at second for the automatic second out, and below, Kelly Gruber applies the tag on Sanders for what looks like the third out, but Umpire Bob Davidson says no.

Opposite, one of several conferences on the mound for Atlanta. Toronto's relievers, including Duane Ward, pitch superbly, but Lonnie Smith is never an easy out. Above, Toronto has several places from which to keep track of the World Series, including (clockwise from top) SkyDome's television production center, a video retailer, one of 70 SkyDome hotel rooms with a view of the field, and the huge video board.

Kelly Gruber, hitless so far in the
World Series, ties Game Three
with a leadoff home run to left in
the eighth inning. But Atlanta
fans remain hopeful.

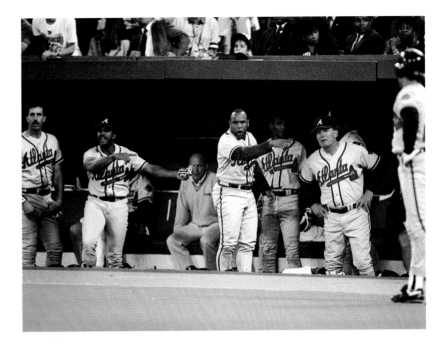

Braves Manager Bobby Cox bounces a helmet off the steps to show his displeasure when first-base Umpire Dan Morrison rules Jeff Blauser went around for the third strike on a check-swing in the ninth inning. Morrison, thinking Lonnie Smith is the culprit, warns the Atlanta bench. When Cox confesses, home-plate Umpire Joe West ejects him.

The maple leaf grows larger as Toronto takes a 2-1 advantage in games. Candy Maldonado sets off a SkyDome celebration by knocking in the winning run in the ninth inning with a fly ball to center field over the head of a drawn-in Otis Nixon.

O Canada!

by Dave Perkins
The Toronto Star

S ay Uncle, Sam. The mouse has roared.
The Toronto Blue Jays marched into Atlanta and became the first team representing a
Canadian city to take the World Series trophy out of the United States.
More than a city celebrated when pitcher Mike Timlin fielded Otis Nixon's bunt and tossed to
first for the final out in the 11th inning of the final game of a stirring, often breathtaking, World
Series. When the great Game Six was done, when the Braves finally ran out of miracles, an entire country
got up and began to dance, sing, pop corks and make other loud noises.

Politely, of course, Canadians being Canadians.

Sometimes, Canadians get angry at the United States. It happens when you sleep with an elephant, as
some call living next door to the U.S. Fly the Canadian maple leaf flag upside down, for instance, as a U.S.
Marines color guard did before Game Two in Atlanta, and Canadians shake their heads over the carelessness.
Many get angry, at least briefly. But mistakes are mistakes and the healing began almost as quickly as the
outraged calls of protest ended. After every official up to and including President George Bush
apologized, Canadian fans finally shrugged and turned their full attention back to baseball.

And it was excellent, entertaining baseball, so good that neither the flag incident nor a couple of bad
calls by the umpires could ruin the show.

In Canada, the World Series often was portrayed as less baseball and more of a Canada-versus-U.S.
showdown. A few Canadians, holding on for dear life to that elusive quality known as perspective, saw it as
our Americans and Latin Americans against their Americans and Latin Americans. Which, technically, it
was, and let's play ball.

There wasn't a Canadian citizen on the field for the Blue Jays—although there are at least 25 honorary
Canadians now. "It may be true that we're all Americans or Latin Americans on this stage," rent-a-pitcher
David Cone told a screaming throng at the Blue Jays' victory celebration in Toronto two days after the
wonderful fact. "But we still feel the pride of Canada. We see the flags. You don't have to be Canadian to
feel that pride. Don't ever change."

Don't ever change? Too late. When it comes to the Blue Jays, in Toronto and in the rest of the country,
everything already has changed. For years, this was the most successful team in baseball that had never
been to the World Series, much less won it. This was the 10th consecutive season the Jays finished with a
won-lost record above .500, by far the longest winning streak in the major leagues.

77

But the best had never been quite good enough.

There had been three previous division championships, in 1985, 1989 and 1991, each one ending in its own inexplicable and/or ignominious defeat. There also had been the greatest final-week collapse in baseball history in 1987, when the Jays frittered away a 3½-game lead by losing their last seven games to hand the division title to Detroit. It was not without justification that the team was known as the Blow Jays—and that was usually the polite term used.

The attitude of the team was altered forever in a 24-hour span last December. The bitter smell of the League Championship Series loss to the Minnesota Twins remained strong in Toronto when Jack Morris, pitching hero of the Twins' Series victory, was signed as a free agent. Before the gleeful shouting had died down, Dave Winfield was added as a free agent to fill the vast void at the positions of both designated hitter and leader of men. With Morris and Winfield, the Jays clearly were aiming high in 1992. Their payroll began the year as one of the top five in baseball, at more than $43 million, then expanded as pitchers Mark Eichhorn and Cone were added in mid-season trades.

There was no glass slipper in this story. This was a team assembled with almost corporate thoroughness in order to win the largest prize available.

From Day One in spring training, Joe Carter, the slugger, and his pal Pat Tabler, the seldom-used back-up first baseman, kept the team focused on the big picture. They designed, bought and distributed T-shirts for every member of the organization. The message was simple:

WE CAN   WE ARE   WE WILL
3 For 3 in 1992

It meant anything less than the A.L. East, A.L. pennant and World Series titles would be a failure.

The East crown, after a season of slogging to 96 wins, was achieved by four games over an obstinate group of Milwaukee Brewers. Along the way, the Blue Jays possessed a 3½-game lead with seven to play. It stood up, of course, and one important ghost no longer haunted the franchise. In the playoffs against the overachieving Oakland Athletics, Toronto's six-game victory exorcised another evil spirit. These were, mostly, the same A's who had humiliated the Jays in the 1989 playoffs. Beating a team managed by Tony La Russa was a large hurdle to clear for the Jays.

The playoff series turned around in Game Four on a ninth-inning home run by Roberto Alomar, the Jays' excellent young second baseman, off none other than 1992 Cy Young Award winner Dennis Eckersley, the greatest relief pitcher of his generation. It was the moment, most Jays later agreed, that confirmed to them that no matter how deep a hole they fell into, they could—and would—dig themselves out.

The World Series, when it arrived, was new ground for the Blue Jays. But it didn't seem a bit shaky, and much of the reason for that was the presence of Jack Morris. The off-season Montana rancher with the reputation as the best money pitcher in baseball had been hired—for $15 million over three years—for this very day. His Toronto-record 21 regular-season wins had been almost glossed over by the fans because this moment, the World Series, was what Morris the Blue Jay was going to be all about.

So, of course, the Braves won Game One, in Atlanta, 3-1 on Damon Berryhill's three-run homer off Morris.

Morris had blown away the Braves in the 1991 World Series, beating them twice and finishing with 13 consecutive shutout innings, including all 10 in that unmatchable seventh game. Morris wasn't bad in this game. He just lost. His out pitch, the forkball, was heading for the dirt with regularity. Through five innings as many baseballs had reached the backstop (one wild pitch) as had reached the outfield.

But in the sixth inning, with Toronto ahead 1-0 on a Carter home run, Morris made his fatal errors. He had been bobbing and weaving around a sudden outbreak of walks until he threw what he would later call "Your basic 390-foot hanging forkball." Berryhill pounced on it for a three-run homer. Morris' World

Series shutout streak against the Braves was abruptly ended after 18 innings. "I guess I needed three or four more innings tonight, didn't I?" he wondered.

Morris reminded the press that Oakland had won the first game of the A.L. playoffs, too. "We'll just regroup and get them tomorrow," Morris said.

At a nearby locker, Ed Sprague cocked an ear, listened and shrugged. Nothing else to say.

Twenty-four hours later, after the flag had been hung upside down in the pre-game ceremonies, Sprague went out and stood the baseball world on its ear. He hit a dramatic two-run, pinch-hit homer in the ninth inning off relief ace Jeff Reardon, producing a stunning 5-4 victory. So instead of wallowing in deep yogurt, down two games, the Jays had captured momentum. They felt they would never give it back and they turned out to be right.

"I didn't see it good," said Sprague, who instead will settle any time for hitting it that way. "I looked up right into the lights. By the time I got to first base, I knew it was gone. It's exciting."

Exciting? Sprague short-changed himself on the adjective. A country watched, disbelieving, and said, "Pinch me."

This home run was Kirk Gibson without the limp. It was one to take its place on the top shelf of the game's dramatic hits. It was only the second time in World Series history that a pinch homer had lifted a trailing team into the lead, Gibson's for-the-ages blast in 1988 being the first. The stunning turnaround also took home plate Umpire Mike Reilly off a large hook, at least in Canada. Reilly made the first terrible call of the Series, somehow missing Roberto Alomar sliding home safely with a vital run after a short passed ball.

Nobody knew it at the time, but in the collision, with pitcher John Smoltz trying to block Alomar off the plate, the Toronto second baseman bruised and sprained his left elbow and wrist. He could barely swing a bat the rest of the series. The damage seemed large enough at the time, especially to Jays' fans.

There is a certain feeling of insecurity, with gusts of paranoia, in many Canadians when it comes to the United States. In baseball, for instance, every bad call by an umpire that goes against the Jays triggers a small brush fire of conspiracy theories that often is difficult to extinguish fully. The umpires, the goofy but popular theory goes, are working for CBS, the network that does not want a Canadian team hanging around killing the post-season TV ratings.

Without Sprague's homer, this fantasy would have gotten a good workout across Canada.

Not that Canadians didn't have other, legitimate reasons to get upset. The upside-down flag had prompted thousands of calls of protest. The embarrassment of Major League Baseball was showing. On full scurry, MLB immediately produced an announcement of apology. So, too, did the Marines. Before Game Three, back in Toronto two days later, threats of mayhem against the Stars and Stripes were common. T-shirts admonishing the Marines or picturing an upside-down U.S. flag sold well.

Hoping to head off further embarrassment, the Blue Jays read a statement, before the national anthems were played in SkyDome, asking for respect for all flags. The Marines, the announcement went, also had "requested the privilege" of carrying the Canadian flag correctly this time. The people responded exactly the way officials had hoped—with decorum—and treated the U.S. anthem properly. The incident suddenly was all but forgotten.

In the top of the fourth inning, something happened that was far more newsworthy—and important. Toronto centre fielder Devon White made what Jays fans will always call, simply, The Catch. The four-time Gold Glove winner turned and sprinted toward the wall, back to the plate, when David Justice lashed a line drive to deep centre.

There were two runners on base in a 0-0 game and both would score on the triple. Except there was no triple. White launched himself up toward the fence and reached out to pluck the ball, backhanded, just before crashing into the padding, face first. "It is definitely in my top 10. I feel I have made better plays," White would say later with a straight face.

No one was required to believe him.

He said he turned and stared at SkyDome's massive replay board: "I couldn't take my eyes off it."

No one could. "That was the play that turned the game around," said Braves Manager Bobby Cox. "Justice hit the ball so hard there was no way that White would get it."

Only he did get it. The Braves' runners, perhaps stunned by what they had seen, got mixed up on the bases and Terry Pendleton passed the runner in front of him for the automatic second out. Deion Sanders, the lead runner, then was trapped off base and run down for the second triple play in World Series history.

Except Umpire Bob Davidson blew the call. It would go into the record books as a double play and as maybe the best Series catch since Willie Mays' immortal snag off Cleveland's Vic Wertz in the 1954 Series. "You don't have to go back to the black-and-white film any more," Dave Winfield said. "You got the best one right here."

"I don't want to take anything away from Willie Mays," White began, when asked to compare himself with the great Giants player.

He took away from Justice, though. He also robbed the Braves and all those who believe triples have a right to life.

Immediately after The Catch, Carter launched a home run for the lead. But the Braves fought back for a 2-1 lead in the eighth inning, the run set up by a Kelly Gruber error. Then, in some kind of immediate appeasement of the baseball gods, Gruber stepped up in the bottom of the eighth and hit a home run, breaking an 0-for-23 streak in the post-season, the longest such piece of futility on record.

Cox had gotten himself ejected from the game in the top of the ninth inning. In the bottom of the ninth, as the Jays built a rally, the Braves used four pitchers, all questionably. The pitching changes were all made by Acting Manager Jimy Williams, former manager of the Blue Jays and immediate predecessor of Cito Gaston, the current string-puller. As manager, Williams was not at all popular with the Toronto fans. But they loved seeing him walk out to the mound repeatedly in his distinctive walk as the inning fell apart on the Braves.

By having Game Two hero Sprague pinch hit for left-handed hitting first baseman John Olerud, Gaston forced the Braves to remove lefty Mike Stanton, their best reliever, after all he did was issue an intentional walk. Gaston's manpower deployment opened the door and the Jays knocked it down. Facing the unfortunate Reardon, Candy Maldonado launched a bases-loaded fly ball deep enough to clear the drawn-in outfield and produce a 3-2 victory for the Jays.

Lefty starter Jimmy Key, a mainstay of the Jays' rotation for several years, would keep the momentum going in Game Four the next night when he got his first post-season start. Key started the game by allowing a ringing single to Otis Nixon, then picked Nixon off first base cleanly. The message was clear: The Braves, who had been running wild on the bases, would not do so tonight against a lefty with an exceptional move to first base. Key began baffling the Braves, throwing strikes (he walked none) and retiring 16 in a row at one point.

His batterymate, catcher Pat Borders, slugged a home run in the third inning for a 1-0 lead. Borders, the eventual World Series MVP, was just quietly going along, hitting in every game, doing his business without a lot of people noticing.

Until the home run, that is. Suddenly, people looked up and saw Borders with a batting average around .500.

The large stolen-base totals against the Jays, by both Oakland and now the Braves, were not the fault of his throwing so much as they were a staff-wide weakness at holding runners close. Borders did what he could about it; he came out early every day for extra throwing practice. That much he can control; fame is another thing entirely.

When emerging from the interview room after Game Four, he confessed he'd never been so scared.

"Did I do all right in there?" he quietly asked a Toronto writer. "Man, I don't like going in there. That's intimidating."

He did fine, of course. So did White, whose RBI single in the bottom of the seventh inning had produced the ultimate winning run in the Jays' 2-1 victory, the one that gave them a 3-1 stranglehold on the World Series.

Afterward, Cox needed to answer tough questions. Like, why did he allow righty Jeff Blauser to bat against righty Duane Ward with two on and two out in the eighth inning while Deion Sanders—the best Braves player in the series—and lefty power bat Sid Bream sat on the bench? Cox said it never occurred to him to pinch-hit, that the Braves were simply unlucky that Blauser's inning-ending ground ball down the first-base line was banged right at John Olerud.

"Why Olerud was playing right there, I'll never know," Cox said.

Blauser said he thought Olerud was out of position, but this was thin soup; the Braves weren't playing well enough to complain about their luck.

Damon Berryhill, the Game One hero, had helped assassinate a potential big inning in the eighth by popping up a surprise bunt attempt with runners on the corners and none out. Berryhill had been 0 for 10 with seven strikeouts since his big home run, and his defensive attitude was showing.

"Maybe they play like that in their league," Key said, "but we don't play like that in our league."

In Toronto, Game Five brought with it some premature (and ill-advised) celebrating. Newspapers boasted "Tonight's the Night," and all day, the radio broadcast the parade route that the city had chosen for the next day.

The Jays were quietly distressed. "We didn't want it announced early," a team spokesman said. "It made us look like jerks."

The Braves, finally getting some offence, took it to Jack Morris—again. Lonnie Smith belted a grand slam in the fifth inning to grease the 7-2 Atlanta win and kill any thoughts of the Jays celebrating on their own field. Afterward, the defiant Morris said he figured the Braves were about finished. "They're in trouble—they're in big trouble," Morris vowed. "They've won two games and I've pitched them both and now I don't pitch again."

Morris was right; two nights later the Braves were in real trouble. They just didn't play like it.

Game Six, easily the best of a good set of games, went into the ninth inning with the Blue Jays nursing a 2-1 lead, achieved on a Candy Maldonado homer in the fourth inning. No Blue Jays reliever had blown a save since July 24, in the season's 96th game. This was the 174th game. Incredibly, though, closer Tom Henke, already the owner of five post-season saves, was nicked for a run on an RBI single by Nixon with two out.

Blue Jays fans everywhere might have collapsed, but the team didn't. Next inning, Gaston called back Key, the Game Four starter. He held the Braves right there until Dave Winfield, the Jays' grand old man and spiritual leader, hooked Charlie Leibrandt's two-out, full-count changeup down the third-base line for a two-run double in the 11th inning. "This is the most fun I've had playing professional baseball," Winfield said later. "I'm almost speechless. I can't even think of the words to describe it."

Others could: It was simply the biggest hit of Winfield's Hall of Fame career, the one that erased forever the "Mr. May" tag George Steinbrenner had put on him in 1981.

It was 4-2 for Toronto at this point and well past midnight on the clock, but the Braves wouldn't stop coming. A leadoff single was followed by a perfect double-play ball rammed at shortstop Alfredo Griffin. But the ball took a wicked bad hop and kicked out into left-centre field. "I'm thinking, 'What kind of haunted house is this?' " Key said. "That's a double-play ball and we're just about out of it. Next thing, the tying runs are on."

Atlanta eventually got one of them home and the tying runner to third base. Mike Timlin, the seldom-used right-hander in the Toronto bullpen, was summoned to face the ever-dangerous Nixon. Before he left the mound after installing Timlin, Gaston warned that Nixon might try to bunt. Nixon bunted the second pitch.

"He not only bunted, he bunted right where Cito said he would," Timlin said later, still half amazed.

The pitcher fielded the ball for the out and the save. It was his first of the season.

Canadian fans will only remember it forever.

GAME FOUR

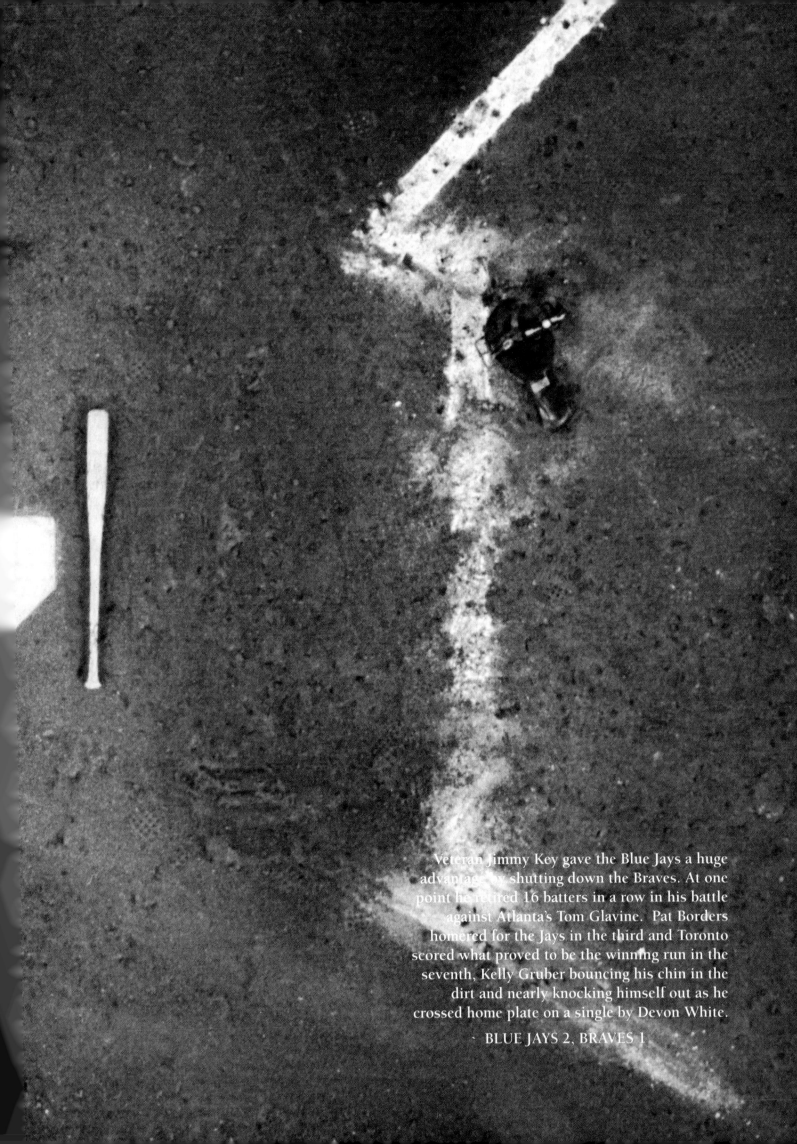

Veteran Jimmy Key gave the Blue Jays a huge
advantage by shutting down the Braves. At one
point he retired 16 batters in a row in his battle
against Atlanta's Tom Glavine. Pat Borders
homered for the Jays in the third and Toronto
scored what proved to be the winning run in the
seventh, Kelly Gruber bouncing his chin in the
dirt and nearly knocking himself out as he
crossed home plate on a single by Devon White.

BLUE JAYS 2, BRAVES 1

America's pastime
becomes Canada's
obsession.

Opposite, Tom Glavine stymies Toronto for the
second straight game, but Jimmy Key (below)
is that much better. Ron Gant pops out in his first
at-bat against Key (opposite, bottom right). Pat
Borders' leadoff home run in the third sails just out
of the reach of Gant in left field, earning Borders a
belly bump from Derek Bell. Lower left, speedster
Devon White searches for another run for the Jays.

Opposite, Mark
Lemke drives in the
Braves' only run in
the eighth. Left,
Duane Ward enters
to get out of the
inning. Below, Dave
Winfield kept getting
on base for Toronto,
this time by forcing
Joe Carter at second
base in the sixth.

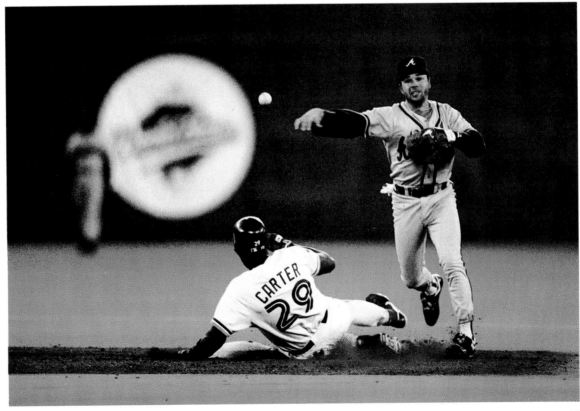

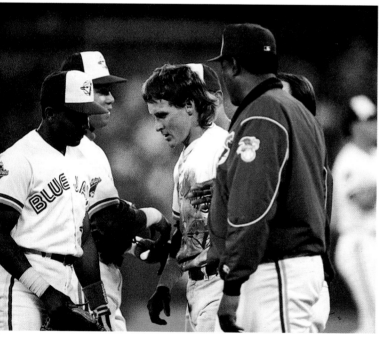

Top, Kelly Gruber suffered through a record-setting hitting drought, but he always played hard—actually knocking himself nearly unconscious while scoring Toronto's winning run in the seventh. Even Braves catcher Damon Berryhill needs a breather after the play at the plate.

The Blue Jays keep their fans
happy in Game Four.

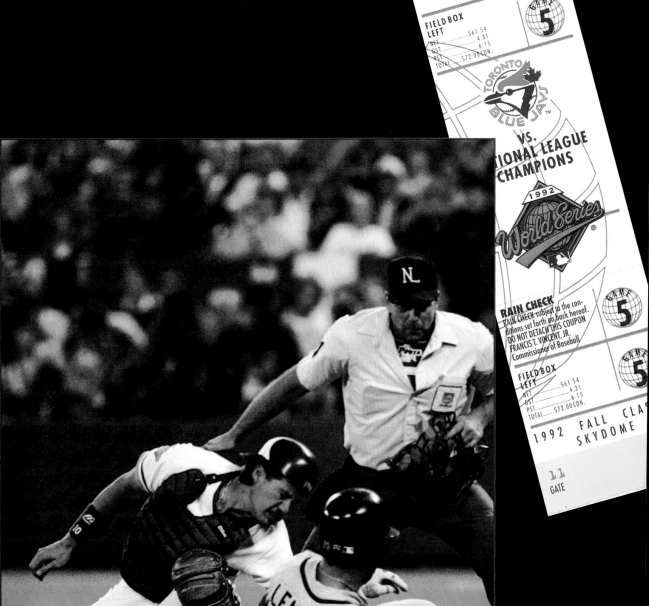

GAME FIVE

SKYDOME, TORONTO
October 22, 1992

"I can't tell you enough how humbling this game is."
—Jack Morris

"TONIGHT'S THE NIGHT" naively proclaimed the headlines in Toronto newspapers. But tonight had to wait. Lonnie Smith sent the Series back to Atlanta and briefly sparked the Braves' fading hopes by slugging an opposite-field grand-slam home run off Jack Morris in the fifth inning. This was the only blowout of the Series and it left Morris 0-3 with a 7.43 ERA in four 1992 post-season games.

BRAVES 7, BLUE JAYS 2

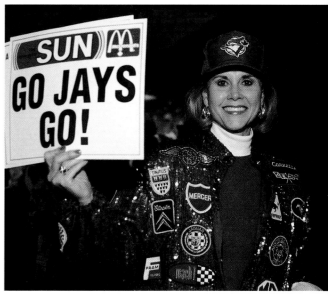

Opposite, author W. P. Kinsella comes to Toronto for his first World Series game. Atlanta starter John Smoltz quietly ponders the challenge of facing his nemesis, Jack Morris, who bested him in 1991's legendary Game Seven. Below, John Olerud scores his first two times up for the Blue Jays, but Atlanta's Otis Nixon matches him.

Toronto's Joe Carter experiences a rare blue moment when Lonnie Smith crushes the big blow for Atlanta with a grand slam in the fifth, only the third bases-loaded home run by a National League player in World Series history.

Kelly Gruber gets a good look at a brushback pitch. Dave Winfield warms up for his Game Six heroics with a single to center in the fifth inning.

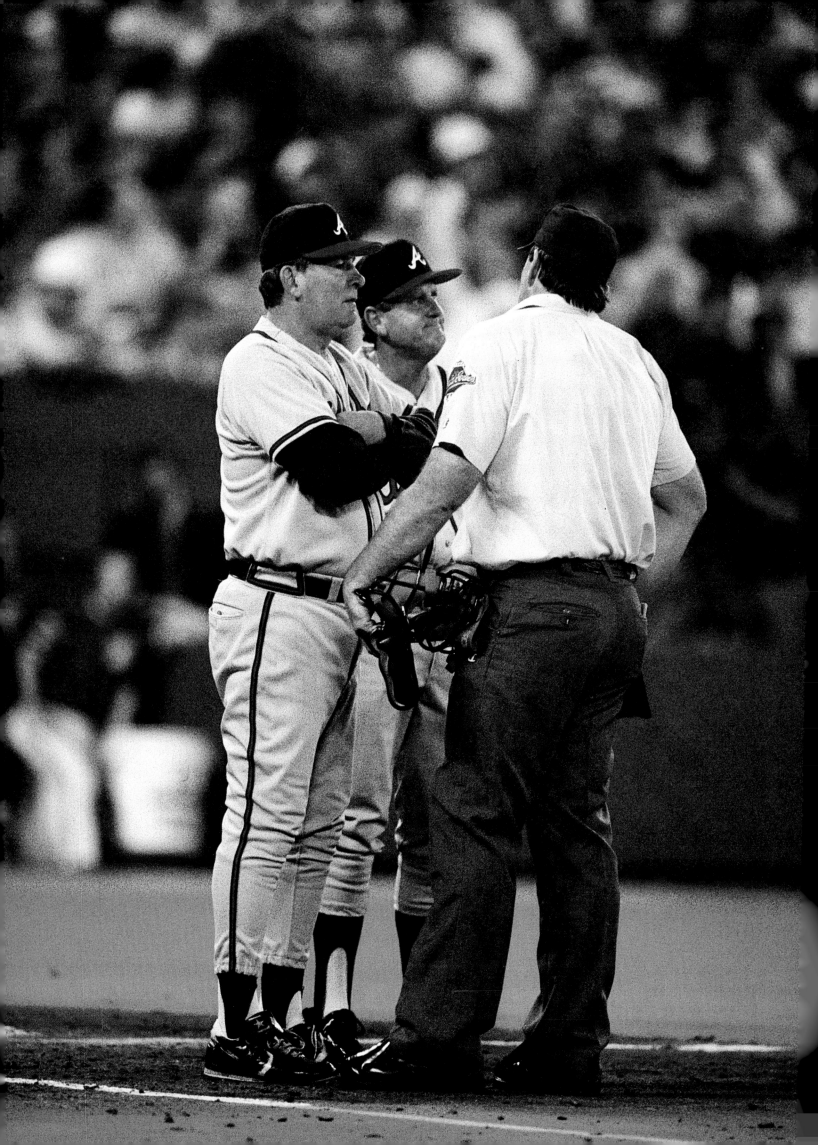

Even with a five-run lead, there's no easing of the tension for Atlanta Manager Bobby Cox and Coach Jimy Williams. Braves pitcher John Smoltz is in command during six innings of work.

Opposite, Atlanta batterymates Mike Stanton and Damon Berryhill know the other players can't hit what they can't see. Mike Timlin tunes up for his important role in Game Six. Manuel Lee can't haul in everything.

Atlanta's Mark Lemke experiences both sides of it, getting thrown out at the plate in the ninth inning but tagging out a Blue Jay at second. Even though Atlanta wins, Toronto still owns the advantage with a 3-2 edge in games.

The World Series bids
a bittersweet farewell
to Toronto, at least
for 1992.

GAME SIX

ATLANTA-FULTON COUNTY STADIUM
October 24, 1992

*"That little base hit gave me my greatest day in baseball.
My best day in baseball with one little stinkin' hit."*

—Dave Winfield

The end of a classic World Series ended with a classic game. Toronto manufactured a 1-0 lead in the first, Atlanta tied it in the third, Candy Maldonado's leadoff homer in the fourth put the Blue Jays ahead, and the Braves tied it in the ninth on Otis Nixon's two-out slap single to left on an 0-2 pitch. Toronto's old man, Dave Winfield, delivered a two-out, two-run double in the 11th for a 4-2 lead, but it wasn't over yet; the Braves pulled to within one run in the bottom half of the inning and had pinch-runner John Smoltz waiting at third with two outs. Nixon, in the hero's slot again, tried to bunt for a base hit but was barely thrown out at first, and Canada celebrated.

BLUE JAYS 4, BRAVES 3 (11 innings)

The World Series returns
to Atlanta.

The fateful Game Six begins, Toronto's David Cone opposing Atlanta's Steve Avery. Damon Berryhill hopes for another big hit. Jeff Blauser laces a second-inning single.

David Justice strikes a blow
for Uncle Sam in the sixth
inning, but it's just a hard
out to right.

In one of the few plays that don't work out for him during this World Series, Pat Borders
is thrown out at the plate by Deion Sanders in the fourth inning.

Clockwise from opposite page, top: The stance remains the same for Sid Bream, Manuel Lee and Umpire Bob Davidson as the play develops. Candy Maldonado gets a high-five from Kelly Gruber after putting Toronto ahead 2-1 with a fourth-inning, leadoff home run. It's never easy keeping Otis Nixon contained on the basepaths. Atlanta reliever Pete Smith comes in for Steve Avery in the fifth inning.

The Braves go through five pitchers in Game Six, including Pete Smith (above) and Mike Stanton (top right). Otis Nixon and Roberto Alomar get one last good look at each other.

Joe Carter offers words of encouragement to David Cone. Dave Winfield whacks away at his undesired 'Mr. May' tag, delivering the winning run with an 11th-inning, two-run double.

Jeff Blauser scores the final two runs for the Braves, in the ninth and 11th innings, but relief pitcher Charlie Leibrandt can't hold Toronto.

With the tying run on third and two down in the 11th inning, speedy Otis Nixon tries to bunt for a base hit. But Mike Timlin's throw beats Nixon to end the game and the World Series, and Joe Carter starts the celebration.

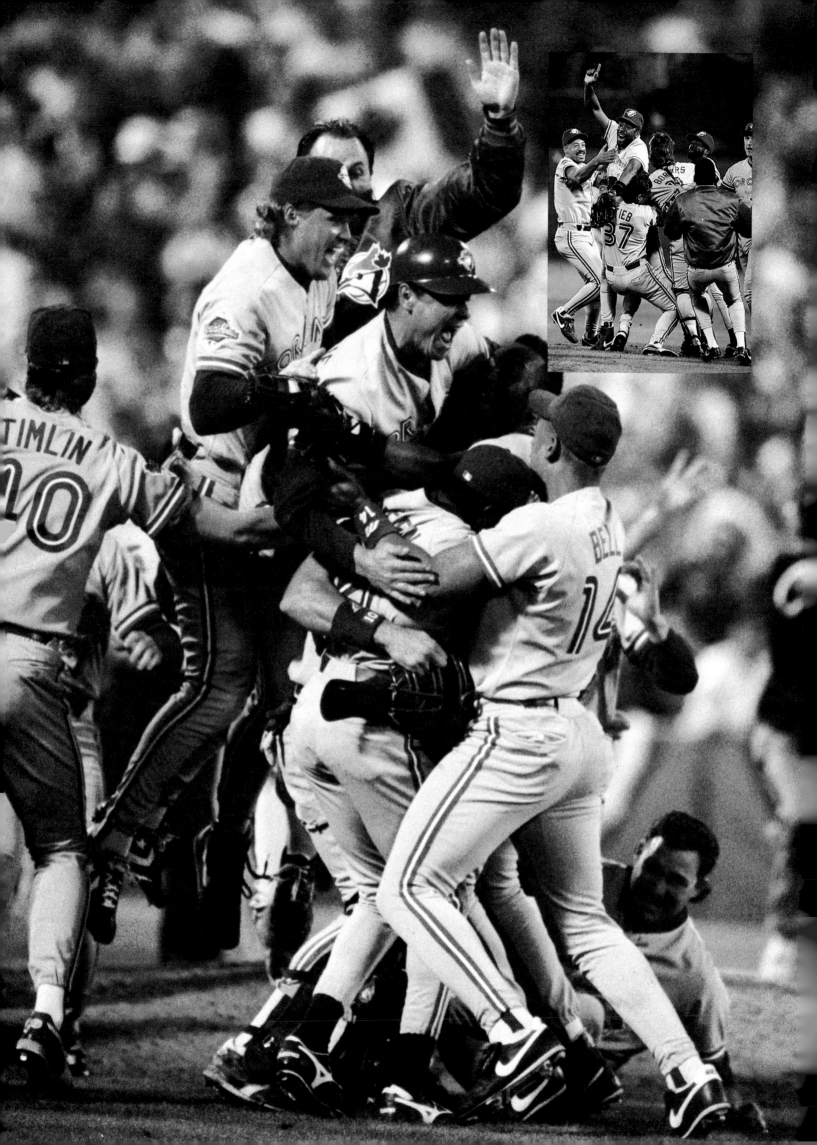

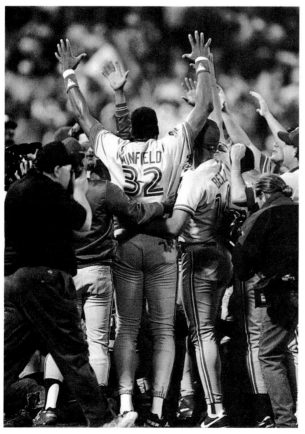

In Toronto, more than 40,000 Blue Jays fans flock to SkyDome to watch Game Six on the huge video screen, then celebrate on the field as soon as the final out is made.

In Atlanta Stadium's visiting clubhouse, bottles of champagne, and years of frustration, were uncorked as the Blue Jays players and their families enjoyed Toronto's first World Series championship.

Dave Winfield and Joe Carter share their glee with announcer Jim Kaat. Pat Borders gets his MVP trophy. Candy Maldonado and Ed Sprague hold court. A wide range of emotions flows through Cito Gaston, but there's nothing left to do but smile as he receives the World Series trophy from A.L. President Dr. Bobby Brown.

EPILOGUE

**TORONTO BLUE JAYS WIN SERIES
FOUR GAMES TO TWO**

"If we had won, we'd be just as happy as they are. But now it's agony. In baseball, there's no in-between."
—John Smoltz

O Canada! O Blue Jays!
Toronto sparkles.

Blue Jays fans feel as tall as the CN Tower. The celebration culminates with a parade to SkyDome.

THE WORLD SERIES IN NUMBERS

GAME ONE

Toronto	ab	r	h	bi
White cf	4	0	0	0
Alomar 2b	4	0	0	0
Carter 1b	4	1	1	1
Winfield rf	3	0	1	0
Maldonado lf	3	0	0	0
Gruber 3b	3	0	0	0
Borders c	3	0	2	0
Lee ss	3	0	0	0
Morris p	2	0	0	0
Tabler ph	1	0	0	0
	30	1	4	1

Atlanta	ab	r	h	bi
Nixon cf	3	0	1	0
Blauser ss	4	0	0	0
Belliard ss	0	0	0	0
Pendleton 3b	4	0	0	0
Justice rf	2	1	0	0
Bream 1b	3	0	0	0
Gant lf	3	1	0	0
Berryhill c	4	1	1	3
Lemke 2b	3	0	1	0
Glavine p	2	0	0	0
	28	3	4	3

Toronto	000	100	000 — 1
Atlanta	000	003	00x — 3

DP-Atlanta1. LOB-Toronto 2, Atlanta 7. HR-Carter (1), Berryhill (1). SB-Nixon (1), Gant (1).

Toronto	IP	H	R	ER	BB	SO
Morris L, 0-1	6	4	3	3	5	7
Stottlemyre	1	0	0	0	0	2
Wells	1	0	0	0	1	1

Atlanta	IP	H	R	ER	BB	SO
Glavine W,1-0	9	4	1	1	0	6

WP-Morris. T-2:37. A-51,763. Umpires-HP, Jerry Crawford; 1B, Mike Reilly; 2B, Joe West; 3B, Dan Morrison; LF, Bob Davidson; RF, John Shulock.

GAME TWO

Toronto	ab	r	h	bi
White cf	5	0	1	1
Alomar 2b	4	1	1	0
Carter lf	3	0	1	0
Winfield rf	4	0	1	1
Olerud 1b	4	0	0	0
Gruber 3b	4	0	0	0
Borders c	3	1	1	0
Lee ss	3	1	1	0
Bell ph	0	1	0	0
Griffin ss	0	0	0	0
Cone p	2	0	2	1
Maldonado ph	1	0	0	0
Sprague ph	1	1	1	2
	34	5	9	5

Atlanta	ab	r	h	bi
Nixon cf	5	0	0	0
Sanders lf	3	1	1	0
Pendleton 3b	4	1	1	0
Justice rf	3	1	1	1
Bream 1b	1	1	0	0
Hunter ph-1b	1	0	0	1
Blauser ss	3	0	1	0
Belliard ss	0	0	0	0
Berryhill c	3	0	0	0
Lemke 2b	4	0	1	1
Smoltz p	3	0	0	0
LSmith ph	0	0	0	0
Gant pr	0	0	0	0
	30	4	5	3

Toronto	000	020	012 — 5
Atlanta	010	120	000 — 4

E-Lee, Bream,Borders. DP-Toronto 2, Atlanta 1. LOB-Toronto 6, Atlanta 8. 2B-Borders, Alomar. HR-Sprague (1). SB-Justice (1), Blauser (1), Sanders 2 (2), Gant (2). SF-Hunter.

Toronto	IP	H	R	ER	BB	SO
Cone	4.1	5	4	3	5	2
Wells	1.2	0	0	0	1	2
Stottlemyre	1	0	0	0	0	0
Ward W, 1-0	1	0	0	0	0	2
Henke S, 1	1	0	0	0	1	0

Atlanta	IP	H	R	ER	BB	SO
Smoltz	7.1	8	3	2	3	8
Stanton	0.1	0	0	0	0	0
Reardon L, 0-1	1.1	1	2	2	2	1

HBP-by Henke (LSmith). WP-Cone, Smoltz 2. T-3:30. A-51,763. Umpires-HP, Reilly; 1B, West; 2B, Morrison; 3B, Davidson; LF, Shulock; RF, Crawford.

GAME THREE

Atlanta	ab	r	h	bi
Nixon cf	4	1	0	0
Sanders lf	4	1	3	0
Pendleton 3b	4	0	2	0
Justice rf	3	0	1	1
LSmith dh	4	0	1	1
Bream 1b	4	0	2	0
Hunter pr-1b	0	0	0	0
Blauser ss	4	0	0	0
Berryhill c	4	0	0	0
Lemke 2b	3	0	0	0
	34	2	9	2

Toronto	ab	r	h	bi
White cf	4	0	0	0
Alomar 2b	4	1	1	0
Carter rf	3	1	1	1
Winfield dh	3	0	1	0
Olerud 1b	3	0	0	0
Sprague ph	0	0	0	0
Maldonado lf	4	0	1	1
Gruber 3b	2	1	1	1
Borders c	3	0	1	0
Lee ss	3	0	0	0
	29	3	6	3

Atlanta	000	001	010 — 2
Toronto	000	100	011 — 3

One out when winning run scored.

E-Gruber. DP-Atlanta 1, Toronto 2. LOB-Atlanta 6, Toronto 5. 2B-Sanders. HR-Carter (2), Gruber (1). SB-Sanders (3), Gruber (1), Nixon (2), Alomar (1). S-Winfield.

Atlanta	IP	H	R	ER	BB	SO
Avery L, 0-1	8	5	3	3	1	9
Wohlers	0.1	0	0	0	1	0
Stanton	0	0	0	0	1	0
Reardon	0	1	0	0	0	0

Toronto	IP	H	R	ER	BB	SO
Guzman	8	8	2	1	1	7
Ward W, 2-0	1	1	0	0	0	2

Avery pitched to 1 batter in the 9th. T-2:49. A 51,813. Umpires-HP, West; 1B, Morrison; 2B, Davidson; 3B, Shulock; LF, Crawford; RF, Reilly.

TORONTO BLUE JAYS

Batting

PLAYER	Avg.	G	AB	R	H	2B	3B	HR	RBI	BB	SO	SB
Roberto Alomar	.208	6	24	3	5	1	0	0	0	3	3	3
Derek Bell	.000	2	1	1	0	0	0	0	0	1	0	0
Pat Borders	.450	6	20	2	9	3	0	1	3	2	1	0
Joe Carter	.273	6	22	2	6	2	0	2	3	3	2	0
Dave Cone	.500	2	4	0	2	0	0	0	1	1	0	0
Alfredo Griffin	.000	2	0	0	0	0	0	0	0	0	0	0
Kelly Gruber	.105	6	19	2	2	0	0	1	1	2	5	1
Jimmy Key	.000	2	1	0	0	0	0	0	0	0	0	0
Manuel Lee	.105	6	19	1	2	0	0	0	0	1	2	0
Candy Maldonado	.158	6	19	1	3	0	0	1	2	2	5	0
Jack Morris	.000	2	2	0	0	0	0	0	0	0	2	0
John Olerud	.308	4	13	2	4	0	0	0	0	0	4	0
Ed Sprague	.500	3	2	1	1	0	0	1	2	1	0	0
Pat Tabler	.000	2	2	0	0	0	0	0	0	0	0	0
Devon White	.231	6	26	2	6	1	0	0	2	0	6	1
Dave Winfield	.227	6	22	0	5	1	0	0	3	2	3	0
TOTALS	.230	6	196	17	15	8	0	6	17	18	33	5

Pitching

PLAYER	W	L	ERA	G	GS	IP	H	R	ER	HR	BB	SO
Dave Cone (R)	0	0	3.48	2	2	10.1	9	5	4	0	8	8
Mark Eichhorn (R)	0	0	0.00	1	0	1.0	0	0	0	0	0	1
Juan Guzman (R)	0	0	1.13	1	1	8.0	8	2	1	0	1	7
Tom Henke (R)	0	0	2.70	3	0	3.1	2	1	1	0	2	1
Jimmy Key (L)	2	0	1.00	2	1	9.0	6	2	1	0	0	6
Jack Morris (R)	0	2	8.44	2	2	10.2	13	10	10	3	6	12
Todd Stottlemyre (R)	0	0	0.00	4	0	3.2	4	0	0	0	0	4
Michael Timlin (R)	0	0	0.00	2	0	1.1	0	0	0	0	0	0
Duane Ward (R)	2	0	0.00	4	0	3.1	1	0	0	0	1	6
David Wells (L)	0	0	0.00	4	0	4.1	1	0	0	0	2	3
TOTALS	4	2	2.78	6	6	55.0	44	20	17	3	20	48

Complete games—None. Saves—Henke 2; Timlin 1.

THE WORLD SERIES IN NUMBERS

GAME FOUR

Atlanta	ab	r	h	bi
Nixon cf	4	0	2	0
Blauser ss	4	0	1	0
Pendleton 3b	4	0	0	0
LSmith dh	4	0	0	0
Justice rf	4	0	0	0
Gant lf	3	1	1	0
Hunter 1b	3	0	1	0
Berryhill c	3	0	0	0
Lemke 2b	3	0	0	1
	32	1	5	1

Toronto	ab	r	h	bi
White cf	4	0	3	1
Alomar 2b	3	0	0	0
Carter rf	3	0	0	0
Winfield dh	3	0	0	0
Olerud 1b	3	0	2	0
Maldonado lf	3	0	0	0
Gruber 3b	2	1	0	0
Borders c	3	1	1	1
Lee ss	3	0	0	0
	27	2	6	2

Atlanta	0 0 0	0 0 0	0 1 0	—	1
Toronto	0 0 1	0 0 0	1 0 x	—	2

DP-Atlanta 2. LOB-Atlanta 4, Toronto 5. 2B-White, Gant. HR-Borders (1).SB-Blauser (2), Alomar (2), Nixon (3).

Atlanta	IP	H	R	ER	BB	SO
Glavine L, 1-1	8	6	2	2	4	2

Toronto	IP	H	R	ER	BB	SO
Key W, 1-0	7.2	5	1	1	0	6
Ward	0.1	0	0	0	0	1
Henke S, 2	1	0	0	0	0	1

WP-Ward. T-2:21. A-52,090. Umpires-HP, Morrison; 1B, Davidson; 2B, Shulock; 3B, Crawford; LF, Reilly; RF, West.

GAME FIVE

Atlanta	ab	r	h	bi
Nixon cf	5	2	3	0
Sanders lf	5	1	2	1
Pendleton 3b	5	1	2	1
Justice rf	3	2	1	1
LSmith dh	4	1	1	4
Bream 1b	4	0	0	0
Blauser ss	4	0	1	0
Belliard ss	0	0	0	0
Berryhill c	4	0	1	0
Lemke 2b	4	0	2	0
	38	7	13	7

Toronto	ab	r	h	bi
White cf	4	0	0	0
Alomar 2b	3	0	0	0
Carter rf	4	0	1	0
Winfield dh	4	0	1	0
Olerud 1b	3	2	2	0
Sprague ph-1b	1	0	0	0
Maldonado lf	2	0	0	0
Gruber 3b	4	0	0	0
Borders c	4	0	2	2
Lee ss	3	0	0	0
	32	2	6	2

Atlanta	1 0 0	1 5 0	0 0 0	—	7
Toronto	0 1 0	1 0 0	0 0 0	—	2

DP-Atlanta 1, Toronto 1. LOB-Atlanta 5, Toronto 7. 2B-Nixon, Pendleton 2, Borders. HR-Justice (1), LSmith (1). SB-Nixon 2 (5).

Atlanta	IP	H	R	ER	BB	SO
Smoltz W, 1-0	6	5	2	2	4	4
Stanton S, 1	3	1	0	0	0	1

Toronto	IP	H	R	ER	BB	SO
Morris L, 0-2	4.2	9	7	7	1	5
Wells	1.1	1	0	0	0	0
Timlin	1	0	0	0	0	0
Eichhorn	1	0	0	0	0	1
Stottlemyre	1	3	0	0	0	1

Smoltz pitched to 1 batter in the 7th.
T-3:05. A-52,268. Umpires-HP, Davidson; 1B, Shulock; 2B, Crawford; 3B Reilly; LF, West; RF, Morrison.

GAME SIX

Toronto	ab	r	h	bi
White cf	5	2	2	0
Alomar 2b	6	1	3	0
Carter 1b	5	0	2	1
Winfield rf	5	0	1	2
Maldonado lf	6	1	2	1
Gruber 3b	4	0	1	0
Borders c	4	0	2	0
Lee ss	4	0	1	0
Tabler ph	1	0	0	0
Griffin ss	0	0	0	0
Cone p	2	0	0	0
Bell ph	1	0	0	0
Key p	1	0	0	0
	44	4	14	4

Atlanta	ab	r	h	bi
Nixon cf	6	0	2	1
Sanders lf	3	1	2	0
Gant ph-lf	2	0	0	0
Pendleton 3b	4	0	1	1
Justice rf	4	0	0	0
Bream 1b	3	0	0	0
Blauser ss	5	2	3	0
Berryhill c	4	0	0	0
Smoltz pr	0	0	0	0
Lemke 2b	2	0	0	0
LSmith ph	0	0	0	0
Belliard 2b	0	0	0	0
Avery p	1	0	0	0
PSmith p	1	0	0	0
Treadway ph	1	0	0	0
Cabrera ph	1	0	0	0
Hunter ph	1	0	0	1
	38	3	8	3

Toronto	1 0 0	1 0 0	0 0 0	0 2	—	4
Atlanta	0 0 1	0 0 0	0 0 1	0 1	—	3

E-Justice,Griffin. DP-Atlanta 1. LOB-Toronto 13, Atlanta 10. 2B-Sanders, Borders, Carter 2, Winfield. HR-Maldonado (1). SB-White (1), Alomar (3), Sanders 2 (5). S-Gruber, Berryhill, Belliard. SF-Carter, Pendleton.

Toronto	IP	H	R	ER	BB	SO
Cone	6	4	1	1	3	6
Stottlemyre	0.2	1	0	0	0	1
Wells	0.1	0	0	0	0	0
Ward	1	0	0	0	1	1
Henke	1.1	2	1	1	1	0
Key W, 2-0	1.1	1	1	0	0	0
Timlin S, 1	0.1	0	0	0	0	0

Atlanta	IP	H	R	ER	BB	SO
Avery	4	6	2	2	2	2
PSmith	3	3	0	0	0	0
Stanton	1.2	2	0	0	1	0
Wohlers	0.1	0	0	0	0	0
Leibrandt L, 0-1	2	3	2	2	0	0

HBP-by Leibrandt (White). T-4:07. A-51,763. Umpires-HP, Shulock; 1B, Crawford; 2B, Reilly; 3B, West; LF, Morrison; RF, Davidson.

ATLANTA BRAVES

Batting

PLAYER	Avg.	G	AB	R	H	2B	3B	HR	RBI	BB	SO	SB
Steve Avery	.000	2	1	0	0	0	0	0	0	0	1	0
Rafael Belliard	.000	4	0	0	0	0	0	0	0	0	0	0
Damon Berryhill	.091	6	22	1	2	0	0	1	3	1	11	0
Jeff Blauser	.250	6	24	2	6	0	0	0	1	9	2
Sid Bream	.200	5	15	1	3	0	0	0	0	4	0	0
Francisco Cabrera	.000	1	1	0	0	0	0	0	0	0	0	0
Ron Gant	.125	4	8	2	1	1	0	0	0	1	2	2
Tom Glavine	.000	2	2	0	0	0	0	0	0	1	0	0
Brian Hunter	.200	4	5	0	1	0	0	0	2	0	1	0
David Justice	.158	6	19	4	3	0	0	1	3	6	5	1
Charlie Leibrandt	.000	1	0	0	0	0	0	0	0	0	0	0
Mark Lemke	.211	6	19	0	4	0	0	0	2	1	3	0
Otis Nixon	.296	6	27	3	8	1	0	0	1	1	3	5
Terry Pendleton	.240	6	25	2	6	2	0	0	2	1	5	0
Deion Sanders	.533	4	15	4	8	2	0	0	1	2	1	4
Lonnie Smith	.167	5	12	1	2	0	0	1	5	1	4	0
Pete Smith	.000	1	1	0	0	0	0	0	0	0	1	0
John Smoltz	.000	3	3	0	0	0	0	0	0	0	2	0
Jeff Treadway	.000	1	1	0	0	0	0	0	0	0	0	0
TOTALS	.220	6	200	20	44	6	0	3	19	20	48	14

Pitching

PLAYER	W	L	ERA	G	GS	IP	H	R	ER	HR	BB	SO
Steve Avery (L)	0	1	3.75	2	2	12.0	11	5	5	3	3	11
Tom Glavine (L)	1	1	1.59	2	2	17.0	10	3	3	2	4	8
Charlie Leibrandt (L)	0	1	9.00	1	0	2.0	3	2	2	0	0	0
Jeff Reardon (R)	0	1	13.50	2	0	1.1	2	2	2	1	1	1
Pete Smith (R)	0	0	0.00	1	0	3.0	3	0	0	0	0	0
John Smoltz (R)	1	0	2.70	2	2	13.1	13	5	4	0	7	12
Mike Stanton (L)	0	0	0.00	4	0	5.0	3	0	0	0	2	1
Mark Wohlers (R)	0	0	0.00	2	0	0.2	0	0	0	0	1	0
TOTALS	2	4	2.65	6	6	54.1	45	17	16	6	18	33

Complete games—Glavine 2. Saves—Stanton 1.

Compiled by the MLB-IBM Information System. Copyright 1992 MLB.

A SERIES FOR THE WORLD
CREATIVE STAFF

Standing, left to right: Mickey Palmer, Michael Zagaris, V.J. Lovero, Ron Modra, Barry Colla, W. P. Kinsella, Laurence J. Hyman. Kneeling, left to right: Michael Bernstein, Beth Hansen, Stephen Green, Jon Rochmis. Not pictured: Furman Bisher, Jon Blacker, David Lilienstein, Dave Perkins, Manny Rubio, Chuck Solomon, Jerry Wachter.

W. P. KINSELLA is best known for his novel, *Shoeless Joe*, which became the hit movie *Field of Dreams*. He has published 11 well-received short-story collections and has won several awards for his work, including the Houghton Mifflin Literary Fellowship Award. He lives in White Rock, B.C.

FURMAN BISHER, of Fayetteville, Georgia, has been sports editor and columnist for the *Atlanta Journal* since 1950. He is a member of the National Sportscasters and Sportswriters Hall of Fame and was the 1987 recipient of the Red Smith Award for long and meritorious service in sportswriting. He has covered every World Series since 1964.

DAVE PERKINS is baseball columnist for *The Toronto Star*. He has been in the newspaper business for 20 years, and lives in Toronto.

LAURENCE J. HYMAN, a resident of San Francisco, is president of Woodford Publishing, Inc., and publisher and creative director of Woodford Press. He served as art director and designer for *A SERIES FOR THE WORLD*.

JON ROCHMIS, of Oakland, California, is managing editor of Woodford Press and Woodford Publishing, and a former Bay Area sportswriter.

JIM SANTORE, of Pleasant Hill, California, is art director at Woodford Publishing.

DAVID LILIENSTEIN, of San Francisco, is marketing director of Woodford Press and a freelance photographer.

DENNIS DESPROIS, of Scottsdale, Arizona, was photography editor for *A SERIES FOR THE WORLD*. He is a freelance photographer and former team photographer for the San Francisco Giants.

STEPHEN GREEN, of Chicago, was chief photographer for *A SERIES FOR THE WORLD*. He is the team photographer for the Chicago Cubs and was the sole photographer of another Woodford Press book, *GOING TO CHICAGO: A Year on the Chicago Blues Scene*.

JON BLACKER, of Toronto, is a freelance photographer who contributes regularly to *The Sporting News*.

BARRY COLLA, of San Jose, California, is a freelance sports photographer and a licensee of Major League Baseball.

BETH HANSEN, of San Francisco, is a freelance photographer and graphic designer.

V.J. LOVERO, of North Tustin, California, is the California Angels team photographer and shoots for *Sports Illustrated*.

RON MODRA, of New York, shoots for *Sports Illustrated* and formerly served as team photographer for the Milwaukee Brewers.

MICKEY PALMER, of Staten Island, owns Focus on Sports, one of the world's largest sports stock photography agencies.

MANNY RUBIO, of Atlanta, is one of the most prominent sports photographers of the Southeast.

CHUCK SOLOMON, of New York City, is a freelance photographer who has published five children's sports books.

JERRY WACHTER, of Baltimore, is team photographer for the Baltimore Orioles, and shoots for Focus on Sports.

MICHAEL ZAGARIS, of San Francisco, is known world-wide for his rock-and-roll photography. He serves as team photographer for the Oakland Athletics and San Francisco 49ers.

PHOTOGRAPHY CREDITS:

Jon Blacker: 12 top right, 60-61, 62 bottom, 63, 73 lower left and middle right, 87 bottom, 94 lower right, 99 top, 110 bottom, 130 top right, middle and bottom, 134, 135, 140 lower left.

Barry Colla: 2 bottom, 28-29 top, 32 inset, 34 left, 46 bottom, 53 top, 74 top, 83, 93 top left, 94 top, 96-97, 103 top, 106 top, 118 top, 123 bottom.

Stephen Green: Front jacket top, middle left, lower left, bottom, 6, 7, 14 bottom left and right, 16 middle right, 17 lower left, 18 center, 30 top right, bottom, 31 top left and right, 34 top, 41, 42-43, 44 top left, 46 top right, 50 lower left, 52 top left and bottom, 53 bottom, 55 top, 56 top and lower right, 57, 64, 68 top, 69 top right, 71 top, 72 lower left, 74 lower left, 75 top left, 76 lower left and right, 86 top right and lower left and right, 89, 93 top right, 94 lower left, 100 top, 101 lower right, 110 top left and right, 112-113, 116 lower right, 119 bottom, 121 bottom, 124 top left and bottom, 125, 128, 129 lower right, 131 top left, middle left and lower left, 141 top.

Beth Hansen: 1, 10 top left and right, 11 bottom, 12 top left, center, 14 top, 15 bottom, 35 lower left, 36 lower left, 45 bottom, 47 bottom, 48 top, 55 lower left, 56 lower left, 62 top, 73 top and lower right, 74 lower right, 87 top, 90 top left, 93 lower left and right, 98, 99 lower left and right, 100 lower right, 109 top left, 115 top right and bottom, 120 left, 133, 138 lower left.

David Lilienstein: 5, 60 inset, 130 top left, 136, 137, 138 top and lower right, 139, 140 top and lower right, 141 bottom.

V.J. Lovero: 70 lower left and right.

Ron Modra: 121 top, 126 top.

Mickey Palmer: 2 top, 25, 26-27, 29 bottom left, 30 top left, 31 bottom, 32, 33 bottom right, 34 bottom, 35 top and lower right, 47 top, 48 lower left and right, 49 top and bottom, 50 top and lower right, 51, 52 top right, 54 58-59, 65 bottom, 69 top left and bottom, 70 top left, 72 lower right, 75 bottom, 76 top left, 90 top right and bottom, 91 bottom, 92 top, 100 lower left, 102 top, 104, 109 top right, 111, 117 bottom, 118 bottom, 120 right, 122 lower left and right, 123 top, 127, 128 inset, 129 top and lower left, 132 top left and right and lower right.

Manny Rubio: 4, 8, 9, 10 bottom, 11 top left and right, 13, 15 top, 36 lower right, 44 top top right and bottom, 45 top and right, 46 top left, 114, 115 top left, 116 top and lower left, 117 top left and right.

Chuck Solomon: Front jacket middle right, 3, 71 bottom, 72 top, 84-85.

Jerry Wachter: 65 top, 66-67, 68 bottom, 70 top right, 75 top right, 88 top and lower right, 91 top, 92 lower left and right, 95, 101 top and lower left, 102 lower bottom, 103 bottom, 105 bottom, 106 bottom, 107, 108, 109 bottom.

Michael Zagaris: 16 top left and right, lower left and right, 17 top left and right, middle left, lower right, 18 top, middle left, lower left and right, 28 bottom left and right, 29 bottom right, 33 top and bottom left, 36 top, 49 right, 54 bottom, 55 lower right, 86 top left, 88 lower left, 119 top, 122 top, 124 top right, 126 bottom.